ANCIENT
ROMAN
MYTHOLOGY

ANCIENT ROMAN MYTHOLOGY

PETER KAMARA

CHARTWELL
BOOKS, INC.

This edition first published in 1996 by
Promotional Reprint Company Ltd.,
Kiln House,
210 New Kings Road,
London SW6 4NZ.

Design and Layout © Promotional Reprint Company Ltd. 1996

CHARTWELL BOOKS, INC.
A Division of BOOK SALES, INC.
P.O. Box 7100
114 Northfield Avenue,
Edison, New Jersey 08818-7100

ISBN 0 7858 0768 3

Printed and bound in China

HALF TITLE PAGE:
The Temple of Neptune at Paestum.
Peter Kamara

TITLE PAGE:
The ruined Forum in Rome. Life File/Mike Evans

CONTENTS PAGE:
A decorative arch on Hadrian's Temple at Ephesus.
Life File/Mike Evans

CONTENTS

The Roman Empire

STRETCHING from Scotland in the north to North Africa in the south, and from the Atlantic coast of Spain in the west to Turkey in the east, the Roman Empire at its height was without doubt one of the greatest enterprises in human civilisation. In an era before mass communication and mechanised transport made travel easy, the Romans controlled an empire that was larger than the modern European Union.

Rome was initially only one of a number of cities that developed in Italy in the ancient world. According to legend, its foundation was ascribed to the twins Romulus and Remus, whose ancestry could be traced back, via the kings of Alba Longa (another of the Italian city states), to Aeneas and thus to Troy. Although there were efforts by Roman historians to determine an accurate date for the city's foundation — Livy, for example, claiming a date of 753BC — these were speculative.

Archaeological evidence suggests that the first permanent settlements in the area now occupied by Rome occurred in the 9th and 10th centuries BC. These were built upon a number of hills that offered natural defensive positions. By tradition Rome was built on seven hills — Aventine, Caelian, Capitoline, Esquiline, Palatine, Quirinal and Viminal — that formed the valley of the River Tiber at this point. The first to be settled were the Palatine and the Quirinal; the two peoples represented by these settlements were the Latins and Sabines of later literary tradition.

Following the foundation of Rome, according to legend, there was a succession of kings; the first was Romulus, who initially shared the throne with Titus Tatius (who was a Sabine), followed by six more culminating in Tarquinius Superbus. He ascended to the throne after killing his father-in-law Servius Tullius. Portrayed as a tyrant, he was expelled from Rome and his departure inaugurated the Roman Republic, which was to last from 6th century BC until the establishment of the empire in the 1st century BC. Although this tradition is certainly mythological, there are grains of truth in that Rome was certainly controlled by the Etruscan kings until the 6th century BC, it was certainly under their control that the various parts of Rome were unified into the single state.

There were a number of significant reforms that occurred during the 6th century BC, many of which are attributed to Servius Tullius. These include the draining of the area that was later to encompass the Forum and the translation of the temple of Diana to the Aventine Hill. Also established at this time was much of the class structure that was to influence Rome throughout much of its history. Although direct Etruscan control disappeared with the expulsion of Tarquinius Superbus, Etruscan influence remained; the great temples to Jupiter, Juno and Minerva on the Capitoline Hill, which were built in the 5th century BC, owed much to continuing Etruscan influence as did many of the religious practices.

With the unitary state Rome gradually started to impose its power over the rest of Latium. At the same time Rome was also developing its own internal structures. The republican constitution comprised three elements — the people, the senate (which had its roots in a council advising the earlier kings), and the magistrates (of which the consuls were the most senior). The people were divided into the patricians and the plebeians and during the early years of the republic were dominated

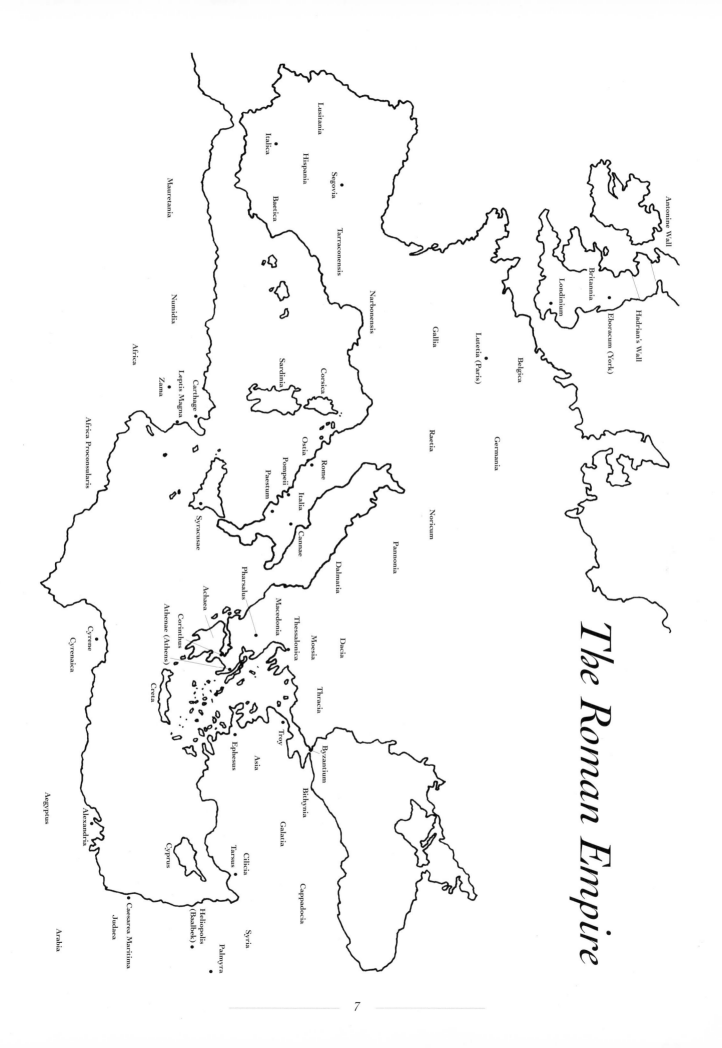

The Roman Empire

internally by the struggle of the latter to be admitted into those positions of power that were controlled by the former.

Over a period of time the plebeians succeeded in gaining access to the highest offices of state. Gradually a new aristocracy, the Nobilitas, emerged; eventually only the highest position in the state, that of Consul, was considered to confer the status of Nobilitas and this led to a small coterie of families that dominated these senior positions. It was not unknown, however, for a non-Nobilitas (eg Cicero) to be elected consul.

The expansion of Rome was not without its setbacks. In the late 4th century BC the Roman army was defeated by the Gauls at Allia, a defeat that resulted in Rome being captured by the victorious army. Gradually, however, over the next few decades Roman power was restored. Control over Latium was regained and by the year 300BC Rome dominated much of central Italy following victories over the Etruscans, Gauls and Samnites.

In the second half of the 3rd century BC Rome was drawn into conflict over southern Italy. This area had been colonised in part by settlers from Greece, and it was the failure of the Hellenistic King Pyrrhus — whose name is recalled by the phrase 'Pyrrhic victory' since he achieved the defeat of the Roman army at Heraclea only at great cost to his own army — to save the Greek settlements that led to their withdrawal.

As the power of Rome grew, so the likelihood of conflict with neighbouring states increased. Dominant to the south of Rome was the Carthaginian empire; Carthage was a city of considerable antiquity located on the north coast of Africa — close to modern Tunis — which had established a formidable mercantile empire covering the African coast from the Straits of Gibraltar to Cyrenaica, southern Spain, Sardinia and Sicily. Through its legendary queen Dido, Carthage played an important part in the foundation of the Roman myth, since it was from Carthage that Aeneas set sail prior to his arrival in Italy.

Initially relations between Rome and Carthage were good and treaties were signed that guaranteed each state's spheres of influence; Roman power over Latium was recognised in return for Roman acceptance of Carthaginian control over Sicily and the western Mediterranean. All this, however, changed when the

BELOW: Aeneas before Dido by Corrado Giaquinto (1703-65). Dido, the Queen of Carthage fell in love with Aenaes and gave him shelter after the sack of Troy. When he eventually left her to fulfil his destiny in Italy, Dido in deepest anguish, threw herself onto a funeral pyre. Christie's Images

city of Messana (modern day Messina) on Sicily sought Roman protection in 264BC. The first Punic War, from 264BC until 241BC, was sparked off by the despatch of a Roman army to Messana. Eventually Carthage was defeated and forced to cede the whole island of Sicily to Rome; later Roman support for revolting mercenaries in Sardinia led Carthage to cede both Sardinia and Corsica to Rome.

The most famous incident of the Punic Wars occurred during the second bout of warfare, between 218BC and 201BC, when the Carthaginian general Hannibal crossed the Alps with his army. Despite his audacity, however, the Carthaginian army was defeated and a further punishing peace settlement transferred control of Spain to Rome. Carthaginian power was further eroded through the loss of its navy, surrendered at the same time as Spain, and by the fact it was forbidden to go to war without the prior agreement of Rome.

Carthage's final humiliation came in 149BC when the third Punic War broke out. Despite its defeat in the second war, Carthage's wealth had increased and it was seen in dispute with its neighbour Masinissa. The dispute was used by Roman leaders, most notably Cato, to agitate for the complete destruction of Carthage, since it was felt that the city still posed a threat to Rome. Cato and his supporters got their way in 149BC when Carthage attacked Masinissa without the necessary Roman authorisation; a Roman army was dispatched and, after a three-year siege, Carthage was razed to the ground in 146BC. With Carthage's destruction, its territories became a Roman province. The city of Carthage was eventually rebuilt and in time grew to become the second largest of all the cities in the western half of the empire.

It was through the defeat of Carthage that Rome gained its first overseas provinces: Corsica, Sardinia, Sicily and Spain, and in 146BC the province of Africa as well. In between the second and third Punic Wars, Roman influence had also been expanding in other directions. The conquest of Cisalpine Gaul — the area of what is now northern Italy to the south of the Alps — was completed in the last decades of the 2nd century BC, whilst between 229BC and the middle of the 1st century BC Rome was involved in a series of wars against the Hellenistic kings that resulted, eventually, in Roman control over Greece and the creation of the province of Macedonia.

The succeeding decades were to see Roman power extended over much of the eastern Mediterranean and the Middle East. The valuable province of Asia was bequeathed to Rome by King Attalus III of Pergamum — the area consisted of that part of western Asia Minor bounded by Galicia and Galatia on the east and by Bithynia in the north. With cities like Pergamum and Ephesus (famous for the temple of Diana) Asia was the wealthiest of all the provinces of the Roman world. Also added to the Roman lands were, amongst others, Cilicia, Bithynia, Cyprus, Crete, Numidia and Syria.

From about 100BC onwards Roman political life was dominated by a number of internecine power struggles that culminated in the civil wars of 49-45BC and 44-42BC. It is during this period that the familiar figures of Julius Caesar, Pompey and Octavian came to prominence. To contemporaries, the fundamental problem was that all of the most influential figures were dominated by their own, rather than the state's, ambition; greed and corruption were rife and personal expectations were not restrained by an increasingly strained constitution. In 60BC Julius Caesar along with Pompey (who had already enhanced his reputation in Spain) and Crassus formed the first Triumvirate; this was never an easy alliance and required rebuilding in 56BC.

In the division of responsibilities, Caesar became Governor of the Province of

Portrait of Julius Caesar by Sir Peter Paul Rubens (1577-1640).
Christie's Images

Gaul. Whilst there he defeated a rebellion led by Vercingetorix at Alesia (a tale familiar to all lovers of the stories of Asterix the Gaul by Goscinny and Uderzo). In addition he also crossed over to Britain, thereby laying the seeds of the eventual incorporation of much of the British Isles into the empire, as well as extending Roman power in Germany. Such were his successes that his prestige and influence in Rome were considerably heightened. In 53BC Crassus, who had been the moderating force in the Triumvirate, was killed by Parthians at Carrhae; his death brought to an end the alliance, with Pompey joining the party of Caesar's opponents.

In order to safeguard his position Caesar, having been declared a public enemy, returned to Rome with his army in 49BC thus precipitating the first of the civil wars. It was on his journey to Rome that Caesar made his famous 'crossing of the Rubicon' — a small river to the north of Rome across which no army was supposed to pass. Pompey fled to the east and Caesar entered Rome in triumph. The threat of Pompey remained, however, and in 48BC Caesar triumphed at the Battle of Pharsalus. Pompey again fled, this time to Egypt, where he was eventually murdered. Caesar, who had by this time received the submission of all the Roman world with the exception of Numidia, followed Pompey to North Africa. There he fell under the spell of Cleopatra, wife of the Egyptian monarch, whose life was to be vividly portrayed later in the Shakespearean play Anthony and Cleopatra. Having spent some time in Alexandria, Caesar undertook a series of actions across the empire to secure Roman power.

Caesar was, without doubt, a man of considerable ambition and skill and his role was central in the creation of the Roman state; but he made the mistake of underestimating the vested interests of his many opponents back in Rome. A conspiracy, of which Caesar was warned by a soothsayer ('Beware the Ides of March'), resulted in his assassination on 15 March 44BC. Amongst the conspirators were Cassius and Brutus. According to Shakespeare, Caesar's last words, as he was stabbed on the steps of the Senate, were 'Et tu, Brute' ('And you, Brutus').

The death of Caesar sparked off the second civil war as Caesar's supporters sought revenge on his assassins. The former were led by Mark Antony, he of the famous 'Friends, Romans, Countrymen' speech, and Caesar's adopted son Octavian, who was 18 at the time. Although their alliance was always strained, the two acted together to ensure the defeat of the murderers. In two battles at Philippi, in Thrace, in 42BC Cassius and Brutus were defeated; Octavian returned to Rome in order to secure the western part of the empire, whilst Mark Antony headed east. Whilst in the west Octavian finally conquered the last of the rebels when he defeated Pompeius Magnus in the battles of Mylae and Naulochus in 36BC. Pompeius fled to Asia where he was murdered by one of Octavian's agents.

Mark Antony, meanwhile, was well-settled in Alexandria; like Caesar before him he had fallen under the charms of Cleopatra and, indeed, had married her. Such was her influence over him that it was easy for Octavian to portray him as a rebel siding with Egypt against the might of Rome and in his arrogance endeavouring to import eastern-style kingship to the republic. Thus Octavian, with the backing of Rome, undertook a military campaign against Mark Antony, which culminated in the naval Battle of Actium in 31BC, in which Mark Antony and his forces were soundly defeated. Humiliated, Mark Antony returned to Egypt, where he committed suicide. With the defeat of Mark Antony's forces, Octavian was able to return to Rome in triumph by adding Egypt to the Roman empire.

It is with Octavian, or Augustus Caesar as he was to become known, that Rome passed from being a republic to an empire. The position that Augustus Caesar held was not officially emperor (since no such position existed within the Roman constitution) but through the various offices that he held (eg Pontifex Maximus — the head of the college of priests and therefore the regulator of all religious practices in Rome) his position was dominant. The army and much of the population owed him allegiance. Under his rule Augustus reorganised a number of the imperial provinces and ensured that the borders were strengthened against outsiders. Although generally speaking the Roman army was well nigh invincible at the time, there were setbacks, in particular one defeat in AD9, forced Augustus to abandon Germany; the borders of the empire were set along the Rivers Rhine and Danube. Beyond those boundaries the various Germanic tribes that were later to be instrumental in the downfall of the western half of the empire were left to their own devices to gradually gain in strength.

The period of the early empire is graphically recounted by Suetonius in his study *The Twelve Caesars* and in Robert Graves reworking of the theme in *I Claudius* and *Claudius the God*. From these works one can get a feel for the intrigue that was rife between the imperial family and amongst the highest echelons of Roman society. Although Rome was in practice an empire with a single autocratic ruler, in theory it remained a republic. There was always the conflict, therefore, between the ambitions of those for whom the imperial purple beckoned and those who believed in either a full restoration of the republic or those opposed to autocratic rule. The problem of hereditary rule was also one that the Roman state never really resolved; although emperors did have natural families, it was not unusual for them also to 'adopt' senior figures as their heir presumptive and this, inevitably, led to strife between the natural and the adopted heirs. Many of the children and other relations of emperors, and their supporters, were to die in peculiar and unexplained circumstances.

Augustus selected Tiberius as his adopted heir in AD4 and, on his death in AD14, the latter achieved the highest office. By inclination, Tiberius, who was 56 on his accession, seems to have been a republican, but this didn't stop him exercising supreme power for more than 20 years — a considerable achievement considering the various plots that were hatched during this period. Ultimately he was to retire to the island of Capri, where, Suetonius alleges, he was involved in some of the worst excesses of sexual deviancy. Tiberius was to die a natural death in AD37, leaving the treasury in surplus — again both of these facts can be considered as significant achievements.

After Tiberius came Caligula. One of the more grotesque figures according to Suetonius, he gained the name, which can be translated as 'Little Boots', from the soldiers of his father's army as a result of spending his early years with the army in Germany and the east. It has been suggested that Caligula suffered from some medical condition that led to his behaviour. Symptomatic of increasing irrationality was his attempt to make his horse a consul. Caligula's short reign came to a bloody end in AD41 after only four years when a conspiracy saw him, his wife and his daughter killed.

AD41 marked a critical date; following the death of Caligula there was much pressure amongst the senate for the full restoration of the republic, but the Praetorian Guard, the elite personal bodyguard of the emperor, sought and found the cowering Claudius and proclaimed him the new emperor. Although Claudius would seem to have been a relatively weak figure — he suffered a great deal of illness as a child — he was a surprisingly successful emperor, particularly in reaction to the excesses of Caligula. It was during the reign of Claudius, for example, that Rome effectively started to colonise the British Isles. He was an effective administrator and also extended the numbers of those entitled to Roman citizenship. He was to die by poison in a plot engineered by his fourth wife Agrippina in AD54. Claudius was the first emperor after Augustus to be deified.

The last of the emperors that had direct links with Julius Caesar was Nero. His 14-year reign started off with promise as he allowed figures like Seneca the Younger to moderate his latent extravagance, but gradually his ambition took over. He poisoned his step-brother Britannicus, in AD59 he arranged for his mother to be murdered, then three years later had his wife Octavia killed following her banishment for adultery. He then proceeded to marry his mistress. It was during the reign of Nero that the persecution of Christians reached its peak, whilst wars in various parts of the empire also weakened the state's treasury. History records Nero as the emperor who fiddled whilst Rome burnt and in AD64 there was a serious conflagration in Rome that many believed Nero himself had started. The last years of his reign were marked by increasing revolt and, when the Praetorian Guard transferred its allegiance to Galba in AD68, Nero was forced to flee. He committed suicide shortly afterwards.

Galba, who was over 70 when he acceded to the throne, had exercised authority under all the emperors from Augustus onwards. He was, however, to prove inadequate for the most important position in the Roman state and was killed in

BELOW: The Arch of Titus in Rome was built to celebrate Titus' conquest of Judea but was only finally completed after his death in AD81.
Peter Kamara

BELOW RIGHT: Street temple in Pompeii. Peter Kamara

January AD69. This same year was to see four emperors. Whilst Galba was being overthrown in Rome by Otho (who was to succeed him), Vitellius had been declared emperor by the legions in Germany. The troops loyal to Vitellius invaded Italy and defeated those loyal to Otho at the Battle of Bedriacum in April. Following this defeat Otho committed suicide. Vitellius arrived in Rome in July, by which stage Vespasian had already been declared emperor of the east. Vitellius was patently inadequate as an emperor and his supporters were defeated at the Battle of Cremona. Vespasian's forces entered Rome in December. Vitellius was captured and executed; ironically, despite the emotions that many of the emperors had raised, Vitellius was the first to die other than naturally or by his own hand.

Vespasian, the last of the four emperors of AD69, was to last slightly longer than his three predecessors, surviving until AD79. Vespasian was a reformer; he reorganised the imperial finances (which resulted in a surplus in the treasury at his death) and the army. In addition he rebuilt many of the major public buildings in Rome (most notably the Forum and the Colosseum). On his death Vespasian was deified and followed by his elder son, Titus, who was to reign for only two years. Despite the brevity of his rule, Titus was regarded as one of the best emperors and was also deified on his death. It was during his reign that the volcano Vesuvius erupted, destroying the cities of Herculaneum and Pompeii; Titus gave generously to assist those displaced by the eruption. He was succeeded by his brother Domitian.

Increasingly Rome was being threatened by the unsubdued tribes from Germany, such as the Huns and the Vandals, and Domitian took active measures to improve the defences of the empire along the Rivers Danube and Rhine, although he also undertook military action that saw Roman influence extended further into Germany. Domitian's reign was to last until AD96 when he was murdered. He had not nominated any successor, which left the Senate free to elevate Nerva into the imperial purple.

Nerva was the first of what are generally regarded as five good emperors; rather than the dynastic succession over the previous 100 years, these emperors generally selected good administrators or generals as their successors. Although he only reigned for less than two years (he died in January AD98), Nerva undertook a number of significant reforms and helped lay the basis for his successors. On his death he was deified. Early on in his reign he adopted Trajan as his heir.

Born in Spain, Trajan was a soldier who reigned for almost 20 years. It was under Trajan that the boundaries of the empire were extended over Dacia and Mesopotamia. The wealth that the successful campaigns brought was used in a series of major building projects, including the construction of his column in Rome that still stands. He died in AD117 and was immediately deified. His successor was Hadrian, who reigned from AD117 to 138. Like his predecessor, Hadrian undertook much building work; of the buildings constructed during this period the most well known include the Pantheon in Rome and his villa at Tivoli. In terms of the empire, Hadrian was a consolidator rather than an expansionist; indeed early in his reign he withdrew from the recently acquired provinces of Mesopotamia, Armenia and Assyria. Hadrian spent much of his reign travelling round the empire inspecting the boundary defences and it was under him that the great wall in

ABOVE: Marble bust of Emperor Hadrian who reigned AD117-138. Christie's Images

northern England that is named after him was started. Hadrian died in AD138 and was immediately deified.

Hadrian's successor was Antoninus Pius. Under Antoninus the Roman empire can be said to have reached its apogee. The treasury was wealthy, there was extensive public building, trade and prosperity increased and, whilst there were continuing military threats at the extremities of the empire, these were relatively limited. It was under Antoninus Pius that Roman influence north of Hadrian's Wall was strengthened, with the building of the Antonine Wall in between the Rivers Forth and Clyde in Scotland; this expansion was, however, short-lived and the empire soon retreated back to the earlier defensive wall. Deified on his death in AD161 Antoninus Pius was succeeded by Marcus Aurelius.

During the reign of Marcus Aurelius, much of the emperor's time was devoted to countering the increasing military threats. In AD166 German tribes invaded and almost reached Italy before being defeated. War was also waged in the east. The cost of the wars weakened the imperial treasury, whilst increasing bureaucracy and centralised power weakened the ability of the provincial leaders to make decisions when external threats grew ever more potent. Finally, the emperor's biggest mistake was to adopt as his successor his son, Commodus, who was unsuitable for the position.

Commodus abandoned his father's policy of war and sued for peace with many of the tribes against whom Marcus Aurelius had undertaken campaigns. Dominated by his Praetorian prefects, Commodus neglected his duties and alienated the senate. He preferred the games, at which he was a regular attendee, rather than duty. He increasingly saw himself as Hercules; indeed was often represented in contemporary statues as a Hercules-like figure. Appalled by the imperial excesses, conspirators arranged for his murder in AD192. He was succeeded by

ABOVE: Marcus Aurelius' statue and temple of Saturn. Although given to contemplation and the quiet life, Marcus Aurelius — who left behind a book of his thoughts —was forced to spend much of his time leading his armies into battle; painting after Giovanni Paelo Pannini and studio.
Christie's Images

LEFT: Hadrian's villa just outside Tivoli. Work commenced in AD126 and was virtually completed by AD134. The complex of palace, libraries, theatres, baths and gardens were designed by Hadrian himself to reproduce the various architectural styles of the buildings he had seen on his travels throughout his empire. Peter Kamara

Pertinax, who had been proclaimed by the Praetorian Guard; he, however, made the fatal mistake of falling out with his sponsors and was murdered by them the following year.

Pertinax was succeeded by Septimus Severus, who had initially been an ally of his. The new emperor quickly undertook the reform of the Praetorian Guard. Apart from the need to establish himself at home, Septimus Severus was also faced by two challengers — Pescennius in the east and Clodius in Britain — and undertook campaigns to defeat both. Under his reign the army was strengthened and much building work was undertaken. He was to die in AD211 at York and was succeeded by his son Caracalla. Caracalla's reign, which was marked first by a purge of his brother Geta and other potential opponents and then by war against the German tribes and Parthia, was relatively short; he was murdered in AD217. He was succeeded by Macrinus, one of those who had conspired in his death. Macrinus, however, quickly lost the support of the army and was deposed the following year and executed. He was succeeded by Elagabalus, who was allegedly the son of Caracalla, whose primary claim to fame was that he was the priest of the eastern sun-god Ela-gabal and introduced the worship of this god to Rome itself. He was to be killed by the Praetorian guard in AD222.

The new emperor was Alexander Severus. Born in AD208, the new emperor was promoted by his ambitious mother. Despite his youth, Alexander Severus was to remain in power until he and his mother were killed by army rebels in AD235. He managed during his reign to reverse many of the excesses of his predecessor, although he was less successful in his military campaigns to defend the imperial boundaries in the east and in Germany.

The death of Alexander Severus marked the start of a period of considerable instability for the empire; over the next 50 years some 13 individuals wore the imperial purple and there were numerous pretenders. This internal upheaval, caused primarily by increasing factionalism within the army, was to weaken the empire considerably at a time when the external threats were growing ever stronger.

It was only with the accession of Diocletian in AD285 that the seemingly irreversible decline in Roman power and prestige was reversed. He introduced wholesale reforms of the administration and taxation systems which radically altered the nature of the empire. During the early years of his reign Diocletian was involved in a number of military campaigns that strengthened his position and eliminated a number of claimants to power. These wars also improved the empire's position in the east.

Bolstered by his early military successes, Diocletian turned his attention to reforming the administration, culminating in a new form of government, the Tetrarchy, in AD293. Under this Diocletian, in overall charge, would rule the eastern half of the empire with Galerius as his assistant, whilst Maximian would rule in the west with Constantius Chlorus by his side. In theory, this would ensure stability, but the new arrangement was to unwind rapidly after Diocletian retired as a result of the ambitions of his successors. Under Diocletian, much new building was undertaken, both in improving the defences of the empire and in Rome. It was also under Diocletian that the final great purge of Christians, begun in AD303, was started. Diocletian retired in AD306, following serious illness, and was to witness before his death in AD316 the unravelling of his administrative structure.

The ambitions of the various claimants to power — such as Galerius, Maximian and Maxentius — led to a series of wars, from which Constantine emerged as victor. He was to rule the empire until AD337 and it was under him that the new capital city, Constantinople, was to be built at Byzantium. During Constantine's

reign Christianity became the official religion of the state, and the new city of Constantinople was not furnished with any pagan temples. Constantine was also a reformer and during his reign the government of the empire was again overhauled and, for a short period, the boundaries were secured through victories over the barbarian tribes. However, the costs involved in the building of the new capital as well as the ever-increasing costs associated with the defence of the empire meant that the empire's finances were weakened.

Constantine was succeeded by his sons Constantius, the second emperor of the name (the first was Constantine's father, who had ruled in the west from AD293-306 under Diocletian), Constantine and Constans. There was strife between the brothers; Constans defeated Constantine (who had held sway in Britain, Gaul and Spain) in AD340 to become sole ruler of the west until he was killed by Magnentius in AD350. Constantius ruled in the east until AD361 having undertaken a purge of many of his relations on the death of his father; during his reign much time was occupied in wars against the Persians and against usurpers (like Magnentius) from the west.

Constantius was succeeded by Julian, a nephew who had survived the purges of AD337 and who had led a rebellion against Constantius just prior to the latter's death. Julian, known as 'the Apostate' because of his secret conversion to paganism, sought to remove Christianity's privileges. In AD363 he set off on a military campaign against the Persians, but was fatally wounded in battle.

In the east Julian was succeeded by Jovian, who reversed his predecessor's anti-Christian policy, but died the following year whilst returning from Constantinople to Rome. He was succeeded by Valentian, who appointed his brother (Valens) as emperor in the east and who undertook a successful defence of the west. Valentian died in AD375 and was succeeded in the west by Gratian,

his son, who had had charge of the western empire from AD367. He was killed by the rebel Magnus Maximus in AD383. Valens ruled in the east from AD364, but suffered a major defeat at the hands of the Visigoths at Adrianople in AD378 and was killed in the battle.

Valentian II, also the son of Valentian, was given power over Italy and Africa by his brother Gratian, but was also defeated by Magnus Maximus. Following the death of Valens in AD378 Theodosius was appointed emperor in the east; he settled with the Visigoths before turning his attention to Magnus Maximus. The rebel was defeated in AD387. Following this victory Theodosius restored Valentian II to power in the east. Theodosius was an ardent Christian and during his reign all pagan worship was finally suppressed. He was also the last emperor to have power over an undivided empire; on his death in AD395 the empire was finally and irrevocably divided — his sons Honorius and Arcadius received the western and eastern empires respectively.

During the latter half of the 4th century AD the empire was facing an ever increasing threat from the westward movement of the barbarian tribes. The potent threat of these tribes had already been demonstrated in AD378 by the victory of the Visigoths at Adrianople; in AD400 the Visigoths under Alaric invaded Italy and sacked Rome in AD410. On the fringes of the empire there was a gradual retreat of Roman domination; Britain, for example, was finally evacuated in AD409. The Burgundians cross the Rhone in the early 5th century and occupied much of eastern Gaul and upper Germany. Simultaneously the Vandals and the Alani crossed the Rhine. In AD415 the Visigoths established a kingdom at Toulouse.

The emperors of the western empire were almost powerless to stop these incursions from the native tribes; they themselves were often no more than the puppets of ambitious generals. There were, however, individual commanders, like Aetius in the mid-5th century, who were able, at least temporarily, to stem the flow of barbarian successes. Aetius defeated the Goths, for example, in alliance with the Visigoths at the Catalaunian Fields in AD451, which helped to ensure that Gaul was secure for a period. However, four years later Rome was again sacked, this time by the Vandals. The last emperor of the west, Romulus Augustus was deposed by a barbarian general, Odoacer, in AD476; there is an irony in the fact that the legendary founder and the actual last ruler of Rome were both called Romulus.

In the east the empire was to survive much longer. It successfully repulsed the barbarian invasions and survived until AD1453 when, weakened by the various Crusades and by the increasing threat of Islam, it fell to the Turks with the sack of Constantinople.

LEFT: The Ruined Forum by Paul Bril (1554-1626) showing the ruins of the Temple of Castor and Pollux.
Christie's Images

Religious Life in Rome

RIGHT and FAR RIGHT: Roman bronze statuettes of Lars — worshipped and revered as one of the guardians of the Roman household.
Christie's Images

RELIGION, whether on a domestic scale or from the standpoint of the state, was one of the cornerstones of Roman society and its exercise was an essential part of the daily life of all Romans. Its importance increased even more with the growth of the cults associated with the imperial family.

Initially, Roman deities were seen as parts of the forces of nature — trees, streams, sea, sun and moon, for example — but as their cults developed so gods became associated with specific attributes. It was under the Etruscans that the so-called 'Capitoline Trio' of Jupiter, Juno and Minerva came to prominence. As in Greece, there was a chief deity, Jupiter Optimus Maximus, and he was supported by a pantheon of lesser deities. Worshippers could select which of the gods was most suitable for their needs. Roman gods lacked the mythological background that the Greek gods possessed — and this makes it difficult to distinguish in part the true nature of the Roman gods because so much of their tradition has been overlaid by the Greek influence — but, in place of the myths, the Romans retained a great belief in ritual.

As the Roman sphere of influence increased, it was inevitable that their existing views about individual cults and myths would become tainted by the religions of the conquered races. Of all the influences, those from Greece were perhaps the most significant. There were Greek colonies on the Italian peninsula — such as Paestum — during the period when Rome was establishing its domestic hegemony, but these were in decline and during the 3rd century BC virtually all Greek power in Italy disappeared. However, in the second half of that century and in the first decades of the 2nd century, when Rome took control of Greece itself, she increasingly exposed the irresistible influence of Greek culture to the empire's domestic population.

There were distinct parallels between the gods of Rome and those of Greece; both had, for example, gods of the sky — Jupiter and Zeus respectively — and of the sea — Neptune and Poseidon — and it was, therefore, easy for the myths and legends to merge and become as one. For the Romans, whose gods had been somewhat primitive, the acquisition of Greece allowed for the Roman gods to inherit the mythological tradition of the Olympian gods; thus, for example, Jupiter was regarded as the consort of Juno just as Zeus was of Hera.

It was not just Greece that influenced Roman religion; throughout the Roman empire existing cults became associated with the Roman deities. In Gaul, for example, the gods Taranis, Teutates and Esus were generally seen as the equivalent of Jupiter, Mercury and Mars, although there were inconsistencies. Rome did, however, often stamp out religious practices that were unacceptable; certain forms of human sacrifice were repressed, for example and in North Africa priests found guilty of human sacrifice were on occasions crucified.

At its most intimate level, religion played an important part in domestic life. Most homes would possess a Lararium — the Lares were the guardian spirits of the household — often in the form of a model temple. The Lares were represented by a statue of a boy holding a saucer in one hand and a cornucopia — the horn of Amalthea exemplifying plenty — in the other. Also worshipped were the Penates, the deities of the storehouse and larder, who, alongside Vesta as the goddess of the hearth, were venerated at meal times.

Just as votive prayers are practised in Christianity — St Jude, the patron saint of lost causes being a particularly common recipient of many — so the Romans directed prayers to their gods. They would often inscribe their vows on wax tablets and attach them to the image of the god being petitioned. If the prayers were answered then the successful petitioner would often make a sacrifice to the god. At the most basic level these sacrifices could take the form of cakes, honey or wine, but animals were also regularly sacrificed, particularly when the occasion demanded it. Certain animals were associated with specific deities; these included an ox for Jupiter, a sheep for Juno and a horse for Mars.

With the rise of the empire there was an additional element in the religious life of the state — the cult of the emperor. It must always be borne in mind that the legitimacy of the position of emperor was suspect and that, through intrigue and ambition, the succession was not automatic. Julius Caesar had already been deified and Augustus regularly styled himself *diui filius* ('son of the god'). In addition, through mythology the imperial family claimed that its antecedents included Romulus and, through him, Aeneas and thus a direct line to the goddess Venus could be claimed.

As part of his efforts to restore the moral fabric of the Roman state Augustus encouraged a revival in the worship of the old gods and the restoration of the temples. Within Rome itself Augustus was careful to ensure that his power was not regarded as godlike — his supposed restoration of the erstwhile republic made such a cult of the personality impossible within the city — but outside it was a different story.

There had been a long tradition in the eastern parts of the empire of ruler worship, and it required little encouragement for a cult of *Genius Augusti* (Augustus's divine will) to emerge. Temples were built to the cult outside Rome; these could be found in places as far apart as Tarragona in Spain, Alexandria in Egypt and Lyons in France. Initially the temples were sanctioned provided that they were dedicated primarily to Roma (the goddess of Rome) with Augustus as the junior partner. Over a period of time, however, the cult of the emperor was gradually subsumed into the Lares, or household gods, so that family prayers would include requests for the welfare of the empire. Just as almost 2,000 years later the British converted Victoria into a Queen-Empress to provide a unifying force to the British Empire, so the cult of the emperor helped to maintain the unity of the Roman state.

Although many of the emperors were to be deified after their deaths, the period of the empire was marked by the growth of two monotheistic religions, both of which had their origins in the east — Christianity and Mithraism. Gradually paganism declined until it was officially prohibited by Theodosius at the end of the 4th century AD, by which time, following the Edict of Milan in AD313, Christianity had become of the official religion of the empire.

THE NATURE OF RELIGIOUS ORGANISATION

There were many aspects to Roman religious life and, given the importance with which religion was viewed, it was inevitable that religious practice would be structured. Some of the cults — which were effectively secret societies, (the Mysteries) — swore their adherents to secrecy, but elsewhere the hierarchy of the Roman state was closely linked to the pagan religions. The following section outlines some of these aspects.

• Fasti: The Romans had a list of those days of the year upon which it was permitted to carry out public business (the *dies fasti*) and those upon which it was forbidden (the *dies nefasti*).

BELOW: Carved stone bust of a satyr — often associated with Pan and Faunus, these creatures are usually shown with the legs and horns of a goat. Christie's Images

• Festivals: Most of the Roman deities had festivals associated with them and which were held either on specific days or during specific periods (with the actual date determined by the magistrates); these were known in Rome as, respectively, the feriae stativae and the feriae conceptivae. These included events like the Lupercalia (to celebrate Faunus), the Saturnalia (Saturn) and the Bacchanalia (Bacchus). These festivals were normally marked with a sacrifice of an animal linked to the deity, and were also times of athletic competition — the Olympic games, for example, were part of a Greek festival in origin — and dramatic productions. Certain of the festivals were particularly noted for the debauchery.

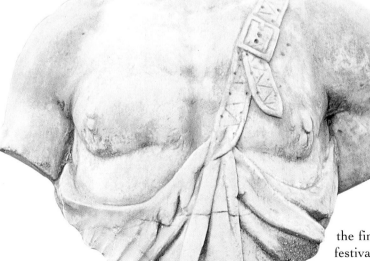

• Fetiales: This was a college of priests who undertook all religious ceremonies involved with war and peace. There were a number of rituals and ceremonies involved; for the declaration of war, for example, a spear was thrown into the ground in front of the temple of Bellona (the goddess of war), this bit of land being seen as a representation of the enemy's territory.

• Flamines: The word *flamen* is the Latin for 'sacrificer' and the Flamines were priests associated with individual cults. Each cult had its own flamen, of which there were 15. Three of the Flamines were *maiores* (major) — those of Jupiter, Mars and Quirinus — and these three were also members of the college of Pontifices. The remainder were *minores* (minor).

• Fratres Arvales: Consisting of 12 members, this was a priestly college that was restored by Augustus. According to myth, the goddess Acca Laurentia was the mother of the first brothers. They celebrated an annual three-day festival each May.

• Lectisternum: This was a religious rite in which it was believed that the gods took part in a feast. It was normally held in a private house, where representations of the gods in question were set by the table.

• Lustration: Ceremonies of purification were an essential part of many Roman festivals. These normally took the form of sacrifices and a procession around the object of the purification; one example of this is the festival of Lupercalia. Every five years, on completing their period of duty, the censors (the Roman magistrates whose tasks included holding the census — the register of Roman citizens and their property) would undertake a ceremony to purify the whole Roman people.

• Pontifices: Religion in Rome was closely linked to the state and a college of priests — pontifex (plural 'pontifices') being the Latin word for priest — was established to ensure the proper observance of all religious activities. The head of the college, the Pontifex Maximus, was a figure of immense power and, amongst other roles, selected the Vestal Virgins. Such was the power of the position that, after the death of Lepidus in 12BC, the post was always filled by the emperor. The official building of the Pontifex Maximus was the Regia, situated at the east of the Forum. It was here that the college of priests met.

• Rex Sacrorum: Second only in seniority to the Pontifex Maximus amongst the Pontifices, the Rex Sacrorum replaced the king (*rex* is Latin for 'king') in ceremonies after the last of the six kings was expelled in 509BC with the establishment of the republic. The Rex Sacrorum undertook many of the official rites.

ABOVE: Bronze examples of the use of the head of Silanus as a decorative motif. Christie's Images

OVERLEAF: Bacchanal by Sir Lawrence Alma Tadema (1836-1912). Dated 1871. Christie's Images

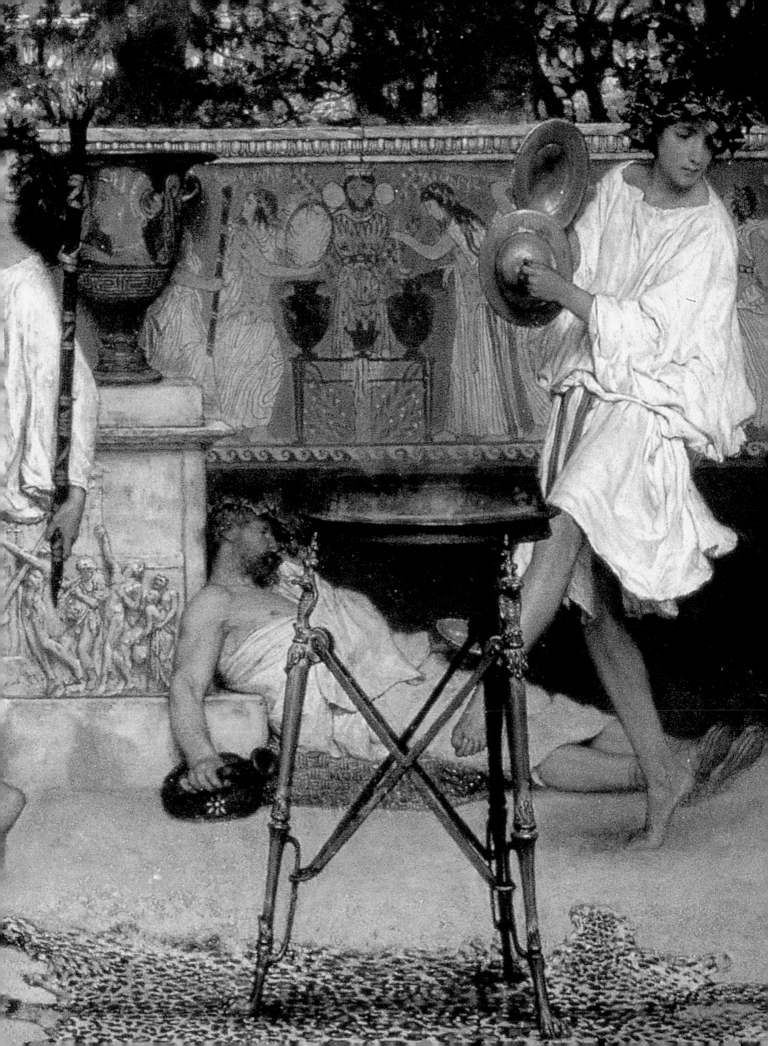

Creation and the Great Myths

THE CREATION MYTH

MOST religions have some form of creation myth and the Romans were no exception. In the period before the world was established all was chaos; the elements of air, earth, fire and sea were all mixed-up. However, god and nature intervened to bring order to this confusion; fire being the lightest, floated upwards and formed the heavens, air formed the next level, followed by earth and then, at the bottom because it was heaviest, came water. With the basic elements now in place, the earth was ordered with rivers and valleys, hills, mountains and fields. Wildlife started to appear and a race of Titans — the offspring of Gaia (earth) and Uranus (heaven) — arrived. One of the Titans, Prometheus, took some of the earth and formed it into the shape of the gods, thereby creating man; whilst all the other animals walked the earth on four legs, looking at the ground, man was to walk on two, thereby looking at the heavens.

Prometheus and his brother Epimetheus were given the task of handing out the skills of life; however, Epimetheus was overly generous with the base animals and had no skills with which to endow man. The situation was rescued by Minerva, who went into the heavens and stole fire, bringing it back to earth. With this man was able to fashion tools and weapons and to introduce trade.

So far there were no women, but in punishment for the unauthorised gift of fire, Jupiter sent Pandora. She was the most beautiful of creatures, endowed by each of the deities with a particular skill or art. She was, however, to find within the possessions of Epimetheus a box containing unpleasant attributes — war, plague, pestilence and so on — which, so long as they were kept in the box were safe. Forbidden to look but overcome by curiosity, Pandora opened the box, thereby releasing these problems into the world.

Initially the world existed in the Golden Age. At this time mankind had no need of law, because right always prevailed and nature always provided. Warfare was unknown and the rivers ran with plenty. The Golden Age was succeeded by the Silver Age, where the seasons first arose and there were extremes of temperature which required mankind to fashion clothes and build houses. As crops would no longer grow automatically, man needed to start to cultivate the ground actively. Then followed the Bronze Age which saw the first threats of war and the first emergence of crime — this caused the earth to become gradually divided amongst the races. The fourth stage, the Iron Age, witnessed the onset of actual conflict as greed took hold. In despair, the gods left the world to mankind's follies.

In anger Jupiter summoned the gods to a council — their route through the heavens being identified by the Milky Way. It was decided that the earth would be relieved of its inhabitants and a new race, more meritorious of the benefits that the earth could bring, would be created. Jupiter and Neptune brought forth a campaign of destruction that saw the earth overwhelmed by sea and storm. The whole of the earth was flooded with the exception of Mount Parnassus leaving only Deucalion and his wife Pyrrha (both Titans) alive. These two had led blameless

ABOVE: Cast iron statue of Hope — all that was left to mankind after Pandora opened Epimetheus' box. Christie's Images

RIGHT: Statue of Jupiter. He was originally a sky god associated with rain and thunder but became the supreme god of the Roman pantheon. Christie's Images

OVERLEAF: Pandora borne to Olympus by Vulcan: Charles Lebrun (1619-90). Christie's Images

lives and Jupiter decided that they would be spared. The pair headed for a temple where they were told by an oracle about how a new race of men would be born. They were to cast stones upon the earth and from theses stone would arise reborn mankind.

THE FAMILY OF THE GODS

Although Jupiter is regarded as the chief of all the Roman deities, he was himself the son of Saturn (Cronos to the Greeks) and Rhea of the race of Titans. In legend, Cronos safeguards his position by eating all his children. Jupiter, however, escapes and leads a revolt against his tyrannical father, which results in the overthrow of the Titans. Cronos is forced to disgorge his children and, following his fall, Jupiter becomes god of the heavens, Neptune the god of the sea and Pluto the god of the underworld. Earth and Olympus were regarded as common possessions upon which all of the gods could have an influence.

Juno was Jupiter's consort and she bore him Vulcan and Mars. Jupiter was also the father of many of the other deities. Juno's jealousy towards Jupiter's other relationships and offspring was a recurring theme through many myths and legends. With Latona, Jupiter fathered Apollo and his twin sister Diana, With Dione, he fathered Venus and was therefore the grandfather of Cupid. Through Maia he was the father of Mercury, through Semele the father of Bacchus. He was also the father of the Hours, the Fates and Astraea (with Themis), of the nine Muses (with Mnemosyne), the Three Graces (with Eurynome), of Proserpina (with Demeter) and of Hercules (with Alcmena). Minerva was another of Jupiter's offspring, although she sprang forth miraculously from his head without an actual mother

THE FOUNDATION STORY

According to Roman legend, the foundation of Rome can be ascribed to Aeneas, a Trojan prince, who after the fall of Troy, fled with his followers westward across the Mediterranean. Initially he makes land in North Africa where he is attracted to the queen of Carthage, Dido, but in order to fulfil his prophesied future he is forced to leave her and sail for Italy. Abandoned and desolate, Dido commits suicide.

There are already established in Italy a number of tribes, one of which, the Latins, welcomes Aeneas. There are varying stories about the relationship between Aeneas and the king of the Latins, Latinus, but the most generally accepted version sees Aeneas marrying Lavinia, Latinus' daughter and killing Turnus, her former betrothed. In the oldest Roman myths, Romulus, the ultimate founder of Rome, was believed to be the son of Aeneas and Lavinia; later versions, however, create a lineage between Aeneas and Romulus to explain the apparent discrepancy in chronology.

In the later versions, Romulus and his twin brother Remus are the sons of Rhea Silvia, the daughter of Numitor, king of Alba Longa, who is deposed by his brother Amulius. To safeguard his position, Amulius makes Rhea Silvia a Vestal Virgin, but she has already conceived the twins — allegedly through the agency of Mars. Following their birth, Amulius casts Rhea Silvia into gaol and throws the twins into the River Tiber. Rather than drowning, the boys are carried ashore where they are found by a she-wolf who suckles them until they are discovered by a shepherd Faustulus. They are then brought up by him and his wife Acce Larentia. They grow to adulthood and kill Amulius thereby restoring Numitor to his throne. Having achieved that, Romulus and Remus depart in order to establish their own

ABOVE: Bronze statuette of Mercury — Jupiter's messenger. Christie's Images

RIGHT: Jupiter and Io. He transforms her into a white heifer to protect her from his jealous wife. Originally a Greek myth, the story was one of many taken up by the Romans and re-interpreted into their mythology. Venetian School. Christie's Images

city. However, Remus is killed in an argument leaving Romulus as the sole founder of the city of Rome.

Having established the city (in, according to legend, 753BC) and its institutions Romulus attracts citizens by kidnapping the Sabine women to provide wives for the incoming men. Peace is, however, ensured between the Sabines and the Romans and Romulus reigns supreme for almost 40 years.

Through the foundation legend, the Romans claimed ancestry from the Trojans and from the gods; these aspects became important particularly in the early years of the empire when the emperors sought to legitimise their position.

FAR LEFT: Jupiter and Danae. This time Jupiter appears as a shower of gold to the imprisoned Danae. The fruit of their union is Perseus. After Sir Peter Paul Rubens. Christie's Images

LEFT: Fragment of a Roman marble sarcophagus depicting the birth of Venus. Christie's Images

LEFT: The Temple of Bel at Palmyra (ancient Tadmor) in Syria, founded in AD32. Bel was an earth deity to the Assyrians and Babylonians. Sited in an oasis in the middle of the desert the temple is rarely seen by anyone except nomads. The locals buried their dead in compartments in the tall towers. Palmyra became a Roman colony in AD212. Life-File/Mike Evans

Who Was Who in Roman Mythology

Acca Larentia One of the minor deities of the Roman world, Acca Larentia's festival was celebrated on 23 December. There are at least two versions as to her role in Roman mythology. In one, she was a rich prostitute who bequeathed her wealth to Rome. In another she was the wife of the shepherd, Faustulus, who brought up Romulus and Remus after they had been cast adrift by their great uncle. According to myth, Acca Larentia was the mother of the first Fratres Arvales; this was a priestly college restored by Augustus.

Acis The lover of Galatea, who was the son of Faunus and a Naiad, Acis was a Sicilian shepherd. Such was the jealousy of the Cyclops Polyphemus, who was also drawn to Galatea, that he chased Acis, forcing Galatea to flee, and killed the youth by throwing a heavy rock, hewn from Mount Etna, at him. Although only a fraction of the stone hit Acis, he was mortally wounded. As his blood flowed, it gradually changed into a river. The fate of Acis is recorded in Handel's opera Acis and Galatea.

Aeneas Expelled from Troy after that city's defeat by the Greek forces under Agamemnon, Aeneas and his followers sailed westward through the Mediterranean. According to legend Aeneas was the son of Anchises and Aphrodite (Venus). He first landed at Carthage, where he fell in love with the city's queen Dido. Their love was, however, fated not to succeed as Aeneas deserted her to fulfil his destiny in Italy. After Aeneas's departure Dido committed suicide. Having arrived in Latium, the district in central Italy from which Rome was eventually to spring, Aeneas married Lavinia, the daughter of Latinus, having killed her previous betrothed, Turnus, in a duel. Aeneas's son, Iulus, was to found the city of Alba Longa, which was the mother city of all the Latin cities. Aeneas was eventually to disappear during a battle whereupon he was raised to the status of god. The dramatic life of Aeneas is recounted in one of the classic tales of Latin literature Virgil's Aeneid.

Ahala In Roman legend, Gaius Servilius Ahala was the commander of the cavalry under the statesman Cincinnatus (in the mid-5th century BC) who defeated Spurius Maelius, a general who was supposed to harbour designs of becoming a tyrant in Rome. To the Romans, the republic that resulted from the expulsion of the tyrannical kings was often perceived as a golden age and many of the emperors, when usurping the throne from their predecessors, often cited the restoration of the republic as a crucial factor in their ambition.

Alaric One of the most potent forces amongst the barbarian tribes were the Visigoths under their leader Alaric. He became chieftain of the tribe at the end of the 4th century AD when the Visigoths still inhabited Thrace; the Visigoths had become a major force within the empire following their defeat of the emperor Valens at Adrianople in AD378. Under Alaric's leadership the Visigoths initially attacked Greece before moving on, in AD401, to attack Venetia. After a defeat in AD408 at Milan by Stilicho, Alaric temporarily retreated, but following Stilicho's death the attack on Italy was renewed. In AD410 the Visigoths captured and sacked Rome. The capture of Rome was regarded by many as an indication of the anger of the gods. Alaric died the same year, whilst leading his army across Italy prior to crossing over to Africa.

Amalthea When Saturn (Cronos) threatened to devour Jupiter (Zeus) as he had all his earlier children, the baby Jupiter was sheltered by Amalthea. The god was kept alive by being fed goat's milk and as a reward she was later placed by Jupiter amongst the heavens. She is often portrayed in art as a goat with a superb pair of horns. These horns — the Cornucopiae — were regarded as symbols of plenty and whoever owned one could be assured of endless food or drink.

Anna Perenna The role of Carthage in early Roman mythology was great. It was from Carthage that Aeneas fled, leaving a distraught Dido. Dido's sister, according to Ovid, was called Anna and after Dido's death she followed Aeneas to Italy. However, she is threatened by Aeneas's wife Lavinia and, being warned in a dream by her dead sister, she again flees. Ultimately she becomes a river goddess and is also associated with vegetation. Her festival — celebrated on 15 March (the first month of the old Roman calendar) — was marked in a grove near Rome. Because of her links to vegetation, she is often associated with Ceres.

Apollo The god Apollo is unique in that he was known by the same name to both Greeks and Romans. This helps to emphasise how far Roman myths were influenced by the earlier colonisation of the Italian peninsula by Greeks. One of the 12 gods of Olympia, Apollo was the god of the sun and light; he was also the founder of the tradition of the oracle at Delphi as he was a god of prophecy as well. His father was Jupiter and his mother Leto (one of the Titans); his twin sister was Diana (Artemis to the Greeks). Apollo and Diana were born on the island of Delos, where their mother fled to avoid the wrath of Juno (Hera). He grew to adulthood miraculously within a few days and departed from Delos to seek his own shrine; he selects Delphi (a place that would remain his principal shrine throughout antiquity), but before he could establish himself there he had to kill the Python, a serpent who was also a daughter of Gaia. In penance for killing the Python, Apollo is banished, one of a number of occasions when he is the subject of the wrath of the other gods. In legend, Apollo helped with the construction of the walls of Troy and always took the Trojan side; given that the Romans believed themselves the descendants of Trojans his continuing popularity amongst the Romans was perhaps inevitable. Apollo, despite being a god of prophecy, is unlucky in love; the nymph Daphne, for example, flees from him, whilst both Hyathincus and Cyparissus are changed into flowers — the hyacinth and the cypress respectively.

Atargatis Known in Rome as *Dea Syria* (the Syrian goddess), Atargatis is an example of a deity from the conquered provinces that continued to have an importance after the Roman take-over. Her cult was widespread in the Middle East (in places like Baalbeck and Damascus), but it also spread through Greece, Egypt and later Italy.

ABOVE: White marble bust of Apollo. The god of light and of the sun. He bears the same name in both Greek and Roman mythology.
Christie's Images

Atlas The Titans were the race of giants that ruled the world before the gods of Olympia. It was Atlas that led the Titans in the war against Jupiter and who was punished by having to bear the weight of the heavens upon his shoulders. He appears in a number of myths. In the labours of Heracles (Hercules), Atlas is temporarily relieved of the pressures of bearing the heavens by being approached by Heracles in his search for the apples of Hesperides.

Attila For almost 20 years, from AD434 until 453, Attila was king of the Huns. The Huns were another of the Germanic tribes that threatened the Roman empire during its dying years. Under Attila's leadership, the Huns held sway over an enormous area of central Europe stretching from the Rhine to the Don. Shortly before his death, he invaded Gaul, but was defeated by an alliance of Aetius (one of the most successful of the latter day Roman generals) and the Visigoths at Châlons. Having weathered that defeat, however, he went on to invade Italy before being persuaded to leave by Pope Leo the Great.

Bacchus The Roman equivalent of the Greek god Dionysius. In Greek myth Dionysius was a relatively important and popular deity; Bacchus on the other hand was widely seen as a symbol of debauchery. His festival was known as the Bacchanalia. Such was the disorder associated with the cult that the senate attempted to suppress in at the start of the 2nd century BC. These efforts, however, failed and the cult remained widespread. The debauchery is reflected in the use of the word Bacchanalian in connection with orgies in English.

Bellona The old Roman goddess of war, who is traditionally associated with the Greek goddess Enyo. She was an important goddess, although her cult was relatively small. Her temple, built in the Campus Martius (the plain stretching from the banks of the River Tiber to the capitol which originally gained its name from the presence of an altar dedicated to Mars), was used by the senate for its meetings outside the sacred lines of the city (the *'Pomerium'*). The temple was also used to welcome ambassadors and victorious generals. In legend she was supposed to prepare the chariot of Mars.

RIGHT: Alliance of Baccus and Cupid by Antoine Coypel (1661-1722). Cupid was the Roman god of love and Baccus a character always associated with drink and revelry. Christie's Images

Bona Dea Known also as Fauna, Bona Dea (good goddess) was the wife(or daughter) of Faunus. Men were excluded from her cult and an annual nocturnal ceremony was held in her honour every December. This ceremony was conducted in part by the Vestal Virgins. The ceremony included the sacrifice of a sow along with much dancing and wine. In 62BC there was a major scandal when Clodius (an important political contemporary of Julius Caesar with whose wife Clodius was having an affair) was caught at the ceremony dressed in women's clothing.

Cacus Another character recorded in the Labours of Hercules, Cacus was a monstrous son of Vulcan and Medusa, who was supposed to be fire-breathing and three-headed. One of Hercules's labours was to return from the west with the cattle of Geryon. His route home took him past Cacus's cave in Italy. Cacus stole part of the herd and, in order to confuse Hercules, dragged the animals backwards so that their hoof prints would indicate that they had gone in the opposite direction. Initially Hercules was taken in by the subterfuge, but alerted by the noise from the hidden animals, he found them and killed Cacus. An alternative version sees Cacus killed by his sister Caca.

Caeculus One of the Roman heroes, Caeculus was in myth the founder of the city of Praeneste. This city in Latium (the modern day Palestrina) was one of the leading cities that fought against Rome in the period when Rome was in the ascendancy. In the empire Praeneste was a fashionable area to build villas and it was also famous for its circular temple to Fortuna Primegenia. In legend, the father of Caeculus was supposed to be Vulcan, who impregnated the hero's mother by issuing a spark of fire which lands in her lap. Praeneste was the home of one of the most important temples to the goddess Fortuna.

Caligula One of the most notorious of the early Roman emperors, Gaius Julius Caesar Germanicus, better known to history as Caligula, was born in AD12. His early life was spent with his father, Germanicus, largely in military campaigns in Germany and the east. After Germanicus's death in AD19 (supposedly poisoned by his wife Agrippina [14BC-AD33]), Caligula returned to Rome where he gradually rose in the favour of the emperor Tiberius. Following the death of Tiberius in AD37 Caligula became emperor. His reign was marked by his increasing irrationality, most notably when he tried to make his horse a consul and by suggestions of incest involving his own sisters. He saw himself as being godlike and his increasing despotism led to his fall. He was murdered in AD41.

Canens The daughter of the god Janus, Canens was a wood-nymph who fell in love with Picus. This relationship inspired the wrath of the enchantress Circe. Picus refused Circe's advances with the result that she turned him into a bird. Canens, seeking desperately her lost lover, pines away leaving only her voice behind.

Carmentis There were a number of Roman deities associated with childbirth. One of them was Carmentis, who, according to legend, was the mother of Evander. Her festival — the Carmentalia — was celebrated in January.

Carna A Roman goddess, Carna ensnared potential lovers by enticing them into a cave. The god Janus, however, is not misled and manages to consummate his relationship with her. In return Carna gains power over the home.

ABOVE: Bust of Gaius Caesar — Caligula, one of the most notorious emperors of all . He reigned AD37-41 and one of his bizarre actions was to make his favourite horse a consul of Rome. Christie's Images

Castores Castor and Pollux (Polydeucus) were twin brothers. Although their mythological background is confused — there are varying stories of their parentage (the sons of either Zeus or Tyndaerus, legendary king Lacedaemon) and adventures — the twins were rewarded for their brotherly love and loyalty by being placed in the heavens by Zeus as the constellation Gemini. The cult of the twins was a relatively early arrival in Latium and a temple, Aedis Castoris, dedicated to them was built, according to Roman legend, at the Forum in 486BC following their role in the Battle of Regillus. The twins, known as the Castores in Rome, were closely associated with horses.

Catamitus Perhaps better known by his Greek name (Ganymede), Catamitus was according to legend the son of the Dardanian king, Tros. When Hera decides to cease to be the cup-bearer to the gods, Jupiter determines to replace her with the beautiful youth. In exchange for Catamitus, Tros receives either a golden vine or a marvellous horse. In one version, Catamitus is carried off to the heavens by a storm, but the most common version sees Jupiter change himself into an eagle and carry the youth heavenwards. The ultimate fate of Catamitus can, perhaps, be best revealed in the fact that the modern English word 'catamite', meaning a boy kept for homosexual purposes, is derived from it.

Ceres Although Ceres, the goddess of crops, can be seen as one of the ancient gods of Rome, her importance became greater once she inherited the mantle of the Greek goddess Demeter. A temple to Ceres was established on the Aventine by 493BC. This was under the control of the aediles (from the Latin *aedilis* the official in charge of streets, markets and the supply of food). The Cerialia, the festival associated with Ceres, was held annually on 19 April.

Comus The son of Bacchus and Circe, Comus was a Roman god of feasts. As the son of Bacchus, he is appropriately portrayed as a young drunkard.

Concordia The Roman goddess of peace.

Constantine Flavius Valerius Constantinus was born in the last quarter of the 3rd century AD. He was the son of Constantius Chlorus who became Caesar of the West in AD293. Constantine joined his father in Britain in AD306 just before the latter's death, after which Constantine was proclaimed emperor by his late father's army. He quickly secured Britain and Gaul before invading Italy. Allied from AD311 with Licinius, who gained control in the east, the pair legitimised Christianity through the Edict of Milan in AD313. Relations between Constantine and Licinius gradually broke down and civil war broke out in AD323. Licinius was soon defeated and committed suicide the following year. Constantine thus became the sole ruler and Christianity became the official religion throughout the empire, although Constantine himself was only baptised on his death bed in AD337. He was also the founder of Constantinople, the 'New Rome' that was destined eventually to rule over the eastern part of the empire and survive the fall of Rome itself. Constantinople (later known as Byzantium and now Istanbul) was to survive until its capture by the Turks in 1453.

Cupid Now one of the most familiar of images derived from classical myths, the bow and arrow-wielding Cupid was the Roman god of love. He is traditionally seen as the equivalent of the Greek god Eros. In one version of the creation legend, Eros is born from Chaos and acts as the bringer-together of the sky and earth

ABOVE: A marble statuette of Cupid, the Roman god of love.
Christie's Images

and is thus seen as a force of nature. Later he was regarded as the son of Vulcan and Venus.

Cybele A classic illustration of the way that provincial cults could be subsumed into the worship of one of the major Roman deities is Cybele. Originating in Phrygia (part of the Roman empire in Asia), Cybele was a mother-goddess who became linked with Rhea. Initially her cult in Rome was conducted by non-Roman priests who were ritually self-castrated before being able to act in the ceremonies associated with the cult. Until the reign of Claudius it was prohibited for Roman citizens to take part in the cult. An annual festival, held between 15 and 28 March, was held in her honour; part of the ceremony included bathing in the blood of a freshly sacrificed bull. In legend, she is believed to have been born with both female and male genitalia, but the threat that this represented meant that the gods castrated her. From the fallen male organs a tree grows, which ultimately causes the pregnancy of a nymph. The resulting child, Attis, is drawn to Cybele but he is unfaithful and ultimately commits suicide. Following Cybele's prayers, Attis's body is not allowed to decay and he therefore becomes a symbol of rebirth and purification.

Cyparissus Much beloved by the god Apollo, Cyparissus was a Greek youth who owned a tame stag. However, the stag is accidentally killed by its owner and in his grief Cyparissus pleads to be allowed to mourn for his loss forever. As a result, Apollo transforms him into a tree — the Cypress.

Diana An ancient Roman goddess initially, closely associated with women, with fertility and with woodland. This last attribution also led her to be regarded as the goddess of hunting. The picture of the bathing Diana (Artemis) being spied on by Actaeon is one of the most familiar in art. In the story, which the Roman goddess inherited from Greek myth, the hunter came upon the naked goddess whilst she was at her ablutions. As a punishment, she transmogrified him into a stag, where-upon he was torn apart alive by his own hounds. One of her most important

BELOW: Sketch of the hunt of Diana. She was the Roman goddess of the woods as well as of women and childbirth. Christie's Images

shrines was reputed to have a runaway slave as priest. The priest was supposed to have killed the previous occupant of the post and would himself face death if challenged by a subsequent runaway.

Discordia Traditionally linked with the Greek goddess Eris, Discordia was the Roman goddess of quarrels. According to Homer, Eris was the sister of Ares. She was also seen as the mother of Killing, War, Hostility and Strife. The most famous myth associated with Eris is that she cast the apple to 'the most beautiful' which Paris awarded to Aphrodite, thereby causing the Trojan war.

Egeria A Roman water-goddess, she is linked with Diana, who changed her into a fountain on the death of the early Italian king Numa, whom Egeria had served as both an adviser and lover.

Evander Allegedly of Greek origin, whose parentage is uncertain — he is possibly the son of Hermes and a nymph or of Echemos (although Carmentis, one of the goddesses of childbirth, is often regarded as his mother) — Evander is in Roman legend an early king of part of Italy, having settled on the Palatine Hill (one of the seven hills that were to form Rome). He has a part in the labours of Hercules when he exonerates Hercules for the death of Cacus. It is to Evander that the introduction of the cult of Hercules to Italy is attributed. There is also a link to the legend of the foundation of Rome, in as much as Evander was still alive when Aeneas reached Italy. Evander assists Aeneas by providing him with soldiers that assist in the suppression of the local tribes. Evander was also believed to have built a shrine to Faunus in the Lupercal cave.

Fauna See Bona Dea.

Faunus Faunus was the grandson of Saturn and the son of Picus and was worshipped as a god of fields and shepherds. He is also seen as a god of prophecy. He is the Roman equivalent of the Greek god Pan. An annual festival — the Lupercalia — with which Faunus was associated was held on 15 February. The ceremony took place at the Lupercal, a cave situated at the foot of the Palatine Hill in which according to legend the she-wolf fed Romulus and Remus. The ceremony was undertaken by the Luperci — young boys who wore nothing save a belt — who wielded whips made of goat skin. After the sacrifice of a goat and a dog, the Luperci beat the bounds of the Palatine Hill. Any bystanders who were whipped were believed to gain improved fertility. Faunus is normally portrayed as half man with the legs of a goat. Linked with Faunus were the Fauns, who were the Roman equivalent of the Satyrs.

The Fates The three Fates, called Clotho, Lachesis and Atropos, were the daughters of Jupiter and Themis (who sat by the throne of Jupiter to give him advice) and controlled the destiny of humanity. They span the thread of mankind's existence and were equipped with shears with which they could cut off the thread when it pleased them. The youngest of the trio was Clotho, who watched over the birth of each individual.

Felicitas A goddess of success who first came to prominence in the mid-2nd century BC when a temple was dedicated to her in recognition of Roman success in the conquest of Spain. Her importance grew with the empire as a means of bringing success to a new emperor and, as such, she often appeared on imperial coinage.

Fides The Latin word *fides* translates as faith, and Fides was a goddess of good faith. Her cult, therefore, was popular and stretched back to the earliest days of Rome. Her figure was often used on coins and, like Felicitas, she became much more important with the rise of the empire as a mark of the loyalty of the army. In ceremonies commemorating her, it was normal practice for the sacrificer to don white gloves, and gloved hands were one of her symbols.

Flora The Roman goddess of flowers who was supposed to have received her first altar from the Sabine king Titus Tatius. Initially she had no festival, but later she was honoured on 28 April when games — the Floriala — were held. The festivities included various elements of debauchery, including coarse mimes. In legend she is originally a nymph (called Chloris) who is pursued by the wind god Zephyr. When the pair marry she is transformed into Flora, from whom springs breath that becomes petals and following whose footsteps grow flowers. In the Roman version of the myths of Juno (Hera), Flora acts following Juno's anger over the birth of Minerva by rubbing herbs on to Juno's stomach with the result that she becomes pregnant and gives birth to Mars.

Fornax According to Ovid, Fornax was a goddess who prevented the harvest of grain from being parched. An annual ceremony — The Fornicalia held during February on a movable date but no later than the 17th of the month — was held in her honour. 17 February was regarded as a festival of the ignorant (*stultorum feriae*) for those who did not know to which branch of the ancient Roman units of population (the *curiae*) they belonged.

Fortuna Fors Fortune was an old Roman goddess, seen as the equivalent of the Greek god Tyche, who was a deity of luck and success. Given her attributes, Fortuna was a popular deity and there were temples to her in many places. At the temple at Praeneste she is called the daughter of Jupiter. She is normally portrayed holding a cornucopia — a horn of plenty — and a rudder — indicating her power to direct lives. On occasions she is shown blindfolded symbolising blind chance.

Furrina Given that the power of Rome lasted for almost 1,000 years it is inevitable that certain deities came and went during that period as new cults appeared. One such casualty was Furrina, who was a prominent deity in the early republic (with her own festival the Furrinalia, held on 25 July), but who had virtually disappeared by the time that the republic was replaced by the empire.

The Furies The Erinnyes or Furies, were the goddesses who punished the crimes of those who had escaped public retribution for their sins. In art the Furies are portrayed with their heads wreathed in serpents. They were called Alecto, Megaera and Tisiphone.

Genius To the Romans each individual had his own genius or power; this concept was eventually developed into a belief that each person had his or her own guiding spirit. This was celebrated on the individual's birthday. Within a household it was the genius of the head of the household that was celebrated. The concept of genius became all the more important with the rise of the empire, as each emperor sought to develop his own cult of the personality.

The Graces The Three Graces, Euphrosyne, Aglaia and Thalia, have been a subject much beloved of artists over the centuries. They were the goddesses that presided over dancing, banqueting and all the elegant arts. Normally portrayed as three beautiful maidens, one of the best-known representations of the trio is in the Canova sculpture that is now to be seen on display at either the Victoria & Albert Museum or in Scotland.

ABOVE: Bronze Hercules. The Greek hero Hercules was popular in Roman culture and many tales were told of his Twelve Labours. Christie's Images

RIGHT: Hercules in the garden of the Hespherides. The Twelfth Labour of Hercules was to steal the golden apples guarded by the Hesperides, nymphs of the evening. Christie's Images

Hercules One of the most famous of all figures in ancient mythology, he was the son of Jupiter and Alcmena (who was a mortal). Juno, who always resented the offspring of Jupiter's relationships with mortals, endeavoured to kill the young Hercules. She sent two serpents to destroy him in his cradle, but he is too powerful and kills them both. However, through her energies, Hercules becomes the vassal of Eurystheus. It is for Eurystheus that Hercules completes his Twelve Labours: they are as follows —

• to kill the Nemean lion. Eurystheus wanted Hercules to bring back the skin of the lion. However, despite using arrows and his club against the monster, Hercules was unable to kill it except through the use of his bare hands.

• to kill the Hydra which possessed nine heads, of which the central one was immortal. Each time a head was struck off, two new ones grew in its place. In order to defeat the Hydra, Hercules was forced to call upon the assistance of his nephew (or servant) Iolaus to cauterise the severed necks before the new heads could grow. The final head was cut off and buried under an enormous rock.

• to capture the hind of Ceryneia. This takes him a year to achieve.

• to capture the boar of Mount Eurymanthus. This was carried out by him returning to Eurystheus with the boar over his shoulders.

• to clean the Augean stables. Augeus, the king of Elis, had a herd of 3,000 cattle, which were housed in stables that had not been cleaned for 30 years. Hercules was able to clean the stables by diverting the course of the Rivers Alpheus and Peneus through them.

• to shoot the Stymphalian birds. These birds plagued the shores of Lake Stymphalus in Arcadia. Hercules scares them into the air through the use of a rattle given to him by Athena. As the birds fly around, Hercules is able to kill them with his bow and arrows.

• to capture the man-eating mares of King Diomedes of Thrace. This he achieves by killing the fire-eating bull that has been attacking Crete.

• to take the girdle of Hippolyte. Hippolyte was the queen of the Amazons, the fearsome race of female-only warriors, from whom the daughter of Eurystheus wanted a girdle. Initially, Hercules is treated well by the Amazons and Hippolyta agrees to hand over her girdle. However, Juno, still smarting from her earlier failures to get Hercules killed, turns the Amazonians against him. Hercules, believing that Hippolyta has acted treacherously, kills her.

• to bring back the cattle of Geryon. Geryon, a monster with three heads, lived in the west (often believed to be a reference to Spain). According to one version of

the legend, as Hercules headed westward, he split a mountain in half, thereby creating the Straits of Gibraltar. Geryon's cattle were guarded by the giant Eurytion and his dog. Hercules, however, managed to kill both and steel the cattle. It was on his return journey eastwards that he encountered Cacus.

• to fetch Cerberus from the Underworld. To achieve this labour, Hercules descended into the Underworld with Mercury and Minerva and got permission from Pluto that Cerberus could be removed temporarily so long as no weapons were used. Despite the strength of the dog, Hercules triumphed and took the dog to Eurystheus before returning the animal as promised.

• to acquire the golden apples of Hesperides. This was in many ways the most difficult of the tasks as Hercules did not know where to the find the apples. These apples were given to Juno as a wedding present from the earth goddess and were entrusted to the care of Hesperus. Hercules's search eventually brings him to Mount Atlas as he believes that Atlas may be able to assist his work, since he was the father of the Hesperides. Relieving Atlas temporarily of the burden to hold up the heavens, Hercules is ultimately successful when the Titan returns with the apples and, with reluctance, resumes his arduous duty.

There are numerous other legends associated with Hercules; for example he was believed to have rescued Theseus from the Underworld. Ultimately, he became one of the immortals, having ascended to heaven, where he married Hebe.

Horatius According to legend, Horatius, who was nicknamed the 'one-eyed' prevented the army of an Etruscan leader, Lars Porsenna, from crossing the Sublician bridge. Once the bridge had been destroyed and Rome thereby saved, Horatius was reputed to have swum across the River Tiber to safety. His exploits were made famous in English in Macaulay's *Lays of Ancient Rome*.

Icelus One of the son of Somnus, Icelus had the ability to imitate birds, beasts and serpents in people's dreams.

Ilia There is more than one myth concerning the birth of Romulus and Remus, the founders of Rome (*See also Rhea Silvia*). Ilia is the daughter of Aeneas and his wife Lavinia. She is loved by Mars, with whom she becomes pregnant. The king of Alba Longa, Amulius, leaves the twins to die on a mountainside, but they are rescued and nurtured by a she-wolf.

Janus Now recorded for posterity in English through the month of 'January', the Latin word *ianus* — the Romans had no letter 'J' — meant covered passage or entrance. Janus was the god of these structures and was always depicted as having two faces; as his importance grew he also became a sky god. A temple dedicated to Janus was located on the north side of the Forum Romanum. It was always considered propitious for battle that the departing army should leave for war through the city's gates in the correct fashion. Janus became associated with the commencement of actions; this was reflected in the fact that from 153BC Januarius became the first month of the Roman year; his festival — the Agonium — was held annually on 9 January. A period of peace was marked by the closing of the temple and the resumption of war by its reopening; needless to say during Rome's turbulent history the temple was closed on only some five occasions. The origins of this aspect of Janus's myth was the result of a belief that he had saved Rome by expelling the Sabines from the Capitol through the use of a powerful stream of hot water.

Julius Caesar One of the most important figures of the late Roman republic, Gaius Julius Caesar was born in July 100BC. A member of one of the main Patrician families, Caesar was destined to lead a political and military life. He proved himself an effective general, extending Roman power in Spain to the Atlantic coast whilst governor there in 61BC. Such was his power that, back in Rome the following year, he, along with Pompey and Crassus, formed the first Triumverate. Caesar again left Rome in 58BC. He was to remain away from the city for the next nine years whilst he subjugated Gaul (effectively modern France) and, in 55BC, launched the first Roman invasion of Britain. In 53BC Crassus, the moderating force within the Triumvirate, was killed and Pompey joined the opposition to Caesar. Tension between both parties increased until war became inevitable. In January 49BC Caesar headed back to Rome with his army, crossing the River Rubicon en route (it was during this crossing that Caesar uttered his immortal phrase *Alea iacta est* — the die is cast). This symbolic act caused consternation in Rome and many of Caesar's opponents fled. Pompey was eventually defeated and by 45BC Caesar had destroyed the last vestiges of Pompey's support. Although Caesar never became king, he was appointed dictator for life in 44BC; monarch in all but name Caesar's domination led to a plot against him. Whilst he was warned of his fate — 'Beware the Ides of March' — the conspiracy against him, led by Cassius and Brutus, was to lead to his murder on 15 March 44BC.

Juno Along with Jupiter and Minerva, Juno was one of a trio of gods that were established by the Etruscans. She was the goddess of women and childbirth and was also the wife of Jupiter. A ceremony, Matronalia, was held annually on 1 March — the month dedicated to Mars, who was Juno's miraculous offspring — in her honour. She is remembered today in the name of the month June. She is often regarded as the Roman equivalent of the Greek goddess Hera and most of the myths surrounding her are derived from that attribution. One exception concerns the birth of Mars. In this version of the legend, Juno is upset following the birth of Minerva directly from Jupiter's head. She is placated when Flora massages her stomach with herbs leading Juno to become pregnant with Mars.

Jupiter Widely regarded as the chief of the gods and was husband of Juno. Now commemorated in the name of one of the planets and in the exclamation 'By Jove', Jupiter (Iuppiter) was the Roman god of the sky. As the supreme god of the Roman pantheon of gods, he can be seen as a direct parallel with the Greek god Zeus. He came in various forms: as Iuppiter Fulgur he was the god of lightning, for example, and as Iuppiter Tonans he was the god of thunder. The most famous of the versions was Iuppiter Optimus Maximus. His cult was based around a temple on the Capitol, which was the model for numerous other temples dedicated to Jupiter throughout the empire. Such was the prestige of the building that returning generals would approach the temple on their knees at the end of their triumphal march through the city. Along with Minerva and Juno, the origins of his cult belong in the Etruscan period.

Juturna A water nymph, Juturna is the sister of the Italian prince Turnus, Juturna aids her brother against Aeneas following the latter's arrival from Carthage. Chased by an infatuated Jupiter, she takes refuge in the River Tiber, but is betrayed. She is given power over rivers and streams in recompense for the loss of her virginity. She continues to protect Turnus until she is receives a warning from Jupiter to abandon him. Ultimately, she descends into a spring in mourning.

BELOW: Baalbeck, in the Lebanon. Today the Greek city of Heliopolis is best known for its Roman monuments. This is the Corinthian Temple of Jupiter. Life-File/Stuart Norgrove

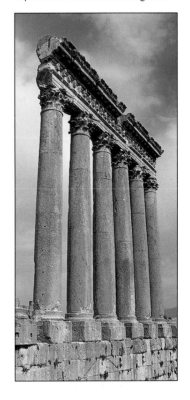

Lara Another Italian nymph, Lara is the daughter of Tiber. She is asked by Jupiter to assist in his pursuit of Juturna, but refuses and betrays him to Juno. In his anger, Jupiter cuts out her tongue and instructs Mercury to deliver her to Hades. However, before he can take her to the Underworld, Mercury falls in love with her. From their union spring the Lares, the minor household gods of Rome.

Latins One of the first settlements to be built in Rome, on the Palatine, was traditionally associated with the Latins, inhabitants from the region called Latium. According to Roman tradition, Alba Longa was the mother city of all the Latin cities and it was only after its destruction that supremacy passed to Rome. The reality would seem to be that Latin power declined whilst Rome was under Etruscan control during the 6th century BC, although it was not until the mid-4th century BC that Latin power was finally destroyed.

Latinus King of the Latins at the time that Aeneas reached Italy. There are various accounts as to his background; he was either the son of Faunus and a nymph or of Circe and Odysseus. In either event he initially welcomed Aeneas and allowed him to marry Lavinia when instructed so to do by an oracle. Lavinia had originally been promised to Turnus, the brother of Juturna, who was eventually killed by Aeneas.

Laverna A very popular deity, Laverna was the Roman goddess of cheats and thieves. One of the city gates to Rome was called the Laverna due to its proximity to an altar dedicated to her worship.

Lemures In Greek mythology, the dead departed the world and entered Hades, the Underworld. The Romans, however, believed that the dead continued to walk the world, disturbing the life of the living. The dead came in two forms — the Lares and the Lemures. The Lares, traditionally seen as household gods (of which each household had one primary god, the lars familiaris), were generally benign. The Lemures were, however, malign. An annual ceremony, the Lemuralia, was held each May in an effort to placate the evil spirits. During the period of the festival, no weddings took place and temples were closed.

Levana The goddess Levana presided over the moment that the newborn baby is first picked up after the midwife has delivered it. In order to prevent any doubts about the legitimacy of the birth, the baby was normally first handled by its father.

Liber The god of fertility was linked with wine and, as with numerous other old Roman gods, was to inherit the mantle of his Greek counterpart, Dionysius. His festival, celebrated on 17 March, was known as the Liberalia and was often the occasion when youths passed from adolescence to adulthood through the adoption of the toga virilis. His cult was associated with those of Ceres and of Libera. Dionysius was also known as Bacchus, and it is from this name that the word Bacchanalian has derived. The festival of Bacchanalia was popular, particularly amongst the lower classes, and was often the source of much drunkenness. This led the senate to try and suppress the cult at the end of the 2nd century BC, but perhaps inevitably the cult was to survive through until the end of the Roman empire.

Libertas The goddess of personal freedom. Following the expulsion of the tyrant Tarquinius Superbus, the last of the seven kings of pre-republic Rome, the state

LEFT: Juno and Argus by Arnold Houbraken. Argus was a giant with 100 eyes whose task was to guard Io while she was a heifer. After he died his eyes were perpetuated by transformation into the peacock's tail. Christie's Images

OVERLEAF: Mars, Venus and Cupid. Their love symbolised to the Romans the triumph of harmony over strife — the god of war is tamed by the love goddess. Christie's Images

acquired 'freedom' or *'libertas'*. The basis of Roman freedom was the republican constitution, although this was much modified over time and much of the opposition to Julius Caesar and the later emperors came from a belief that imperial power ran counter to the liberty enshrined in the constitution. To many Romans, appalled by the excesses of certain emperors, the republic represented a golden age to which the state should return.

Libitina Just as the Romans had gods who looked after their entry into the world (*See Levana*), so too did they have deities who looked after their death. Libitina was the goddess who watched over funerals.

Luna The goddess of birth and of the moon. She was worshipped at a number of temples, including one on the Aventine Hill that was burnt down during the reign of Nero (he who fiddled whilst Rome burnt). Luna is the equivalent of the pre-Greek goddess Selene and of the Greek Artemis. In myth Selene was the sister of Helios and Eos, and like her siblings was the possessor of a chariot on which she drove across the sky. There are various myths related to Selene. In one she falls in love with Endymion and, after bearing him 50 daughters, has him put into everlasting sleep so that she can continue to enjoy his beauty. Selene is also (with Zeus as the father) the mother of Herse (dew) and Pandia. Selene was also linked amorously with Pan.

Maia The Roman goddess of growth after whom the month of May was named. Her festival was celebrated on 1 May with a sacrifice. She is occasionally confused with the Greek mythological figure of the same name who was the eldest of the Pleiades — the daughters of Atlas — who was the mother of Hermes.

Manes Mention has already been made of the Lares and Lemures as spirits of the dead. The Manes represent an alternative version, which saw the spirits of the dead as a collective and single deity. This god watched over places of burial and could be placated by sacrifice. Just as Christian burials use an abbreviation RIP (*Requiescat in pace* — Rest in peace), Roman graves used an abbreviation DM, which stood for *Dis Manibus Sacrum*. Roman poets used the word Manes to indicate the realm of the dead. Towards the end of the Roman empire, there was a shift in the use of the word away from the collective to represent the soul of an individual.

Mars To the Romans, the god Mars was regarded as the legendary father of the twins Romulus and Remus. He was primarily the god of war, although in this role he was gradually supplanted by Minerva, but also had agricultural connections. His name is commemorated by the month March, which was the first month on the Roman calendar (hence September was the seventh month — from the Latin for seven Septem — and October the eighth, etc). It was usual practice for a Roman general to go to the Regia, where the Pontifex Maximus had his official building, to make offerings to Mars prior to departing for war. The woodpecker and the wolf were both sacred to Mars. As the premier god of war he was a parallel to the Greek god Ares and thus shared many of the myths that had descended from the Greek cult. However, given his importance in the foundation myth, Mars has a

Bronze winged Mercury on a pedestal He was a popular figure with Romans and as well as being a messinger, he had particular significance for new works, stemming from the Roman tradition of dedicating the first fig from a fig tree to Mercury.
Christie's Images

much greater importance to Rome than Ares did to the Greeks. An example of this can be seen in the belief that he gave the Romans a sacred shield that would protect them; in order to confuse potential thieves the Romans then manufactured a further 11 which they hang in the temple dedicated to Mars.

Matuta Matuta was a minor Roman goddess of growth. Her annual festival, the Matralia, was celebrated on 11 June. According to some sources she was also a goddess of the dawn.

Mercury The god of trade, known as Mercurius, was the Greek god Hermes adopted by Rome. He shared with Hermes the winged cap and shoes as well as the herald's staff. It would appear that his cult had no roots in the earliest days of Rome; certainly he lacked both a festival and a flamen (priest). In that he seems to have closely resembled the parallel Greek god he is similar to both Ceres and Diana. A temple to him was established in 495BC. Its foundation date, 15 May, was also the day when the festival of traders was held.

Minerva The third of a trio of gods whose cult was established by the Etruscans, Minerva was the goddess of arts and crafts and was thus a parallel with the Greek goddess Athena. Her festival was held on 13 June. Like her Greek counterpart, Minerva also had a warlike character and as such she gradually supplanted Mars. She is often portrayed wearing a helmet.

Mithras Inevitably, as the empire expanded, it came into contact with gods and cults from those races and nations that it conquered. Some of these religions, most

BELOW: Minerva awakes Endymion. He had been put into a perpetual sleep by the moon goddess Selene who fell in love with him and couldn't bear the thought of him dying. Circle of Anton Kern (1710-47). Christie's Images

ABOVE: Marble relief of Mithras.
Christie's Images

notably Judaism, survived the Roman assault, whilst others were subsumed into existing practices. There were, however, a number of cults that became adopted by the Romans and traces of which can be found throughout the empire. Of these the most famous is the cult of Mithras. Mithras was the Indo-Persian god of light and Persian immigrants brought the cult to Asia Minor, via Mesopotamia, in the pre-Roman era. It was not to thrive in the region until the dominance of Rome, however. According to the Roman historian Plutarch, pirates from Cilicia (situated on the south-east coast of Asia Minor) were well practised in the cult. With its many bays and natural harbours, Cilicia was an area renowned for piracy and Rome undertook many missions to suppress them. One such mission was led by Pompey in 67BC, one of the most influential military leaders of the last decades of the Roman republic.

From the first century AD the cult of Mithras spread rapidly. Members of the cult, who could only be men and many of whom were soldiers, had to go through seven stages of initiation from Raven (Corax) to Father (Pater). Ceremonies were held in secret and the temples were often small, although ceremonies could also be held in caves and underground.

The legend of Mithras was based around his miraculous birth from a stone and his various adventures. These included combat with the sun-god, with whom Mithras came to be closely associated. His most important adventure was in hunting down and killing a mysterious bull; the symbol of the death of the bull is repeated in temples and carvings associated with the cult. To members of the cult, the killing of the bull was the triumph of the god over evil and death. Like Christianity, the cult of Mithras offered salvation through the rebirth of immortals. The cult of Mithras reached its peak at the end of the 3rd century AD. By that date, however, the rise of Christianity was becoming inexorable and, following the Edict of Milan in 313AD (which recognised Christianity), the cult of Mithras gradually declined alongside the military power of Rome that had been its cornerstone.

Morpheus The son of Somnus (Hypnos) and thus the brother of Icelus and Phantasus. He is a personification of dreams who inhabits the Caves of Sleep. Morpheus played a central role in the myth of Halcyone, whose husband Ceyx (king of Thessaly) was killed at sea. Halcyone waits for her husband's return, ignorant of his fate until Morpheus, adopting the pose of the dead Ceyx, brings news of his death. The following morning, she goes to the sea shore from where she watched her husband depart and is transformed into a bird. Halcyon is an alternative name for the kingfisher.

The Muses The Muses, of whom there were nine in number, were the daughters of Jupiter and Mnemosyne (memory). Each of them had a particular area of art or science to control: Calliope was the muse of epic poetry; Clio that of history; Erato that of love poetry; Euterpe of lyric poetry; Melpomene of tragedy; Polyhymnia of sacred music; Terpsichore of song and choral dance; Thalia of comedy; and Urania of astronomy. Calliope was the mother of Orpheus (the father was Apollo) and she is normally portrayed holding a book and crowned with laurels. Clio is also portrayed with a book, in which she records the acts of the heroes. Erato is regarded as the inventor of the lute and the lyre and is normally portrayed as being crowned with roses and myrtle. Euterpe was regarded as the inventor of all wind instruments.

Mysteries Many of the ancient cults of classical society were secret societies, into which only the initiated — known as the mystai — could enter. Initiation rites were often graded and each initiate had to advance from one stage to the next. A number of the eastern cults adopted by the Greeks and Romans, such as that of Cybele and Mithras, were primarily secret in organisation. Little is known about the actual ceremonies, as they were held in secret and only the initiated could attend. Those who revealed the secrets of the Mysteries were liable to punishment.

Narcissus Although primarily a Greek mythological figure, one version of the life of Narcissus was described by Ovid. In this the nymph Echo dies of grief after having been rejected by Narcissus. Echo had been punished by Juno with the loss of speech; she pines away to nothing but a voice. Narcissus was a beautiful youth who was condemned to fall in love with his own reflection in the water. Thinking that the reflection is a water-spirit he bends over to kiss it. The reflection disappears but, as he backs away, it reappears. Like Echo, Narcissus dies of pining for an impossible love. The nymphs prepare a funeral pyre for him, but when searching for his body they are unable to find it; all that is left is a flower of white and purple — the narcissus.

Neptune From about 400BC Neptune became the Roman equivalent of the Greek god Poseidon as the sea god and, therefore, the inheritor of those myths

LEFT: Triumph of Neptune: Frans Franken II. Christie's Images

ABOVE: The Temple of Neptune at Paestum. So called from the 18th century because of its size, in fact later excavations prove it to be dedicated to Hera. One of the best preserved of all ancient sites, Paestum was a Greek colony in Italy founded c700BC. Designed in the 5th century BC, the Doric temple is nearly 60m long and 24m wide.
Peter Kamara

around the life of Poseidon were adopted. Prior to that date Neptune appears to have been simply the god of fountains, water and streams. Neptunalia was his festival; it was held annually on 23 July. Like Neptune he is normally portrayed clutching a trident and being carried in a chariot formed of a sea-shell drawn by dolphins or sea-horses

Nero   Famous as the emperor who fiddled whilst Rome burnt, Nero Claudius Caesar succeeded his adoptive father Claudius in AD54, the latter having been poisoned by the former's mother Agrippina (who had married Claudius in AD49). Agrippina (AD15-AD59) was the daughter of the earlier Agrippina. Initially Nero seems to have been a model emperor, but he was soon to be involved in plots to eliminate those that he perceived as threatening his position. His step brother, Britannicus (the son of Claudius), was poisoned in AD55 and his mother was assassinated in AD59. In AD53 Nero had married Octavia, the daughter of Claudius (and thus his step-sister), but she was divorced and eventually murdered in AD62. Nero's position was undermined by costly wars in Britain and Parthia and by the execution of many of the leading figures of Roman society (whose wealth Nero then confiscated). It was alleged he was directly responsible for the fire in AD64 that destroyed much of Rome. He was also one of the main persecutors of the new religion, Christianity. A plot to topple him in AD65 failed, leading to the death of many of the conspirators including the writer Petronius, who committed suicide by cutting his own wrists and then binding the wounds so that his death was long drawn out. Eventually, rebellion forced Nero to flee from Rome and he was to commit suicide in AD68.

Octavius (Augustus Caesar)   Adopted as his son by Julius Caesar in 44BC, Gaius Octavius was 18 when Caesar was murdered. Despite warnings to the contrary, he sought to avenge the murder and, along with Marcus Antonius (Mark Antony), plunged Rome into a second civil war. Following the deification of Julius Caesar in 42BC Octavius became a god's son. In a series of campaigns between 43 and 37BC most of his opponents were defeated; in this campaign he was assisted by Marcus Antonius, but it was not long before conflict between the erstwhile partners developed. Following their successful campaign in the east Marcus Antonius had based himself in Alexandria where he fell under the spell of Cleopatra. Octavius used Antonius's increasing infatuation with Cleopatra, along with the Antonius's testament (which bequeathed his estates to Cleopatra's children), as a means of quelling this threat to the empire. Antonius and his supporters were defeated at the Battle of Actium. Octavius was able to complete the conquest of Egypt whilst Antonius committed suicide.

As with his adoptive father Octavian was never formally called king or emperor, although he established positions of power within the Roman hierarchy that meant that he was able to control affairs of state and religion. In 27BC he was granted the title 'Augustus' and the eighth month of the year was renamed in his honour. Under his rule the borders of the empire were both strengthened and extended, although he was finally forced to abandon Germany in AD9 and delineate the empire's borders as running along the Rivers Danube and Rhine. He died in AD14 and was within days deified. He was succeeded by Tiberius.

Palinarus   The journey from Troy via Carthage to Italy was a dangerous one and Aeneas was fortunate to have Palinarus as the helmsman of his ship. So successful is he at guiding the ship safely through the storms sent by Hera after their departure from Carthage that she sends the god of sleep, Somnus, to cause him to fall asleep at the tiller. Falling overboard, Palinarus is washed ashore and killed by the local population. Later the spirit of Palinarus begs Aeneas to be allowed to cross the Styx, but the request is refused as he has never received a proper burial.

Pantheon It was normal in Greek and Roman religions to supplement an entreaty to an individual god with an appeal to all of the gods. The word 'Pantheon' is derived from the Greek words for all (*pan*) and god (*theos*). There still exists in Rome a temple, called the Pantheon, which has its origins in the 1st century BC when it was built for Agrippa. It was called the Pantheon because it had altars to many of the gods and, being circular, was believed to represent the sky. The building that survives today is largely the work of the Emperor Hadrian.

ABOVE: Detail from the Temple of Hadrian at Ephesus.
Life-File/Andrew Ward

Pax Following his victory in the civil war after the murder of Julius Caesar, Augustus dedicates an altar to Pax, the goddess of peace. Reflecting the benefits that peace can bring, the goddess is depicted holding an olive branch and carrying a cornucopia (or horn of plenty). As with a number of other Roman deities, the word Pax was also used in the Latin language and words derived from it are still used in the English language.

Penates A second group of minor household deities were the Penates. They gained their name from the Latin word penus, which translates as store cupboard or larder. The Penates of the Roman state were treated with particular reverence as they were believed to descend from Aeneas and thus had been carried by him from the burning ruins of Troy.

Picus According to legend, Picus was the father of Faunus and thus, in one version of the myth, the grandfather of Latinus. As with a number of these more obscure figures, there are variants to his life, although there are common elements. In one version, he is a pastoral god who has the power to change shape. He becomes a woodpecker, which was a bird sacred to Mars. An alternative version sees him changed into a woodpecker through the actions of Circe, whom he has spurned in favour of Canens, a nymph.

Priapus Priapus was a god of fertility whose cult spread to Greece following the conquest of the Hellespont by Alexander the Great. His cult also spread to Italy. According to the Greek legend he was the son of Dionysius (Bacchus) and Aphrodite. His mother, however, rejects him due to his misshapen body and huge phallus. The donkey, believed to be the symbol of lust, was sacred to him and donkeys were sacrificed to him. Since he is a grotesque figure he is often used as a scarecrow and thus became a protector of gardens. Obscene verse was often written about him or dedicated to him.

Pluto The Roman equivalent of the Greek god Hades. In Greek myth Hades was one of the three sons of Cronos (Saturn) — the other two were Zeus (Jupiter) and Poseidon (Neptune) — who, on the defeat of his father, received the Underworld as his realm. He kidnaps Proserpina and makes her his queen. In Greek myth, the Underworld is approached over the River Styx with the dead being ferried by the ferryman Charon. Once the deceased reach the Underworld, they are judged by Minos, Rhadamanthys and Aeacus. The most wicked are sent to Tartarus, the lowest level of the underworld. The dead are prevented from returning to the earth by the dog Cerberus. Although it is difficult for the living to enter the realm of the dead and return alive, there are a number of stories — such as Orpheus in the underworld and Hercules' removal of Cerberus as one of the 12 labours — where this is achieved.

Pomona Pomona was the Roman goddess of gardens and fruit trees. She attracts the attention of Vertumnus, the god of the seasons, who appears to her in a variety of guises (as a shepherd, a fruit-picker and as a tender of vines) but on each occasion his advances are rejected. Finally, he appears as an old woman to plead his case and Pomona finally succumbs.

Proserpina Known to the Greeks as Persephone, Proserpina was the daughter of Ceres (Demeter) and Zeus. She was abducted by Pluto (Hades) and transported to the Underworld. Finally Pluto and Ceres reach an agreement whereby she spends half the year on earth — reflected in the seasons spring and summer — and half the year with her husband in the Underworld — the seasons of autumn and winter. Her abduction and rape by Hades has been a popular theme in art.

Psyche The story of Psyche is a relatively late addition to the myths and legends of the Roman gods and is one of the few cases where a known Roman writer has extended the literature of the gods. According to Apuleius, Psyche was one of three daughters of an earthly king. Two of the daughters are plain, but Psyche has such beauty that the population desert the worship of Venus. This, inevitably, angers the goddess, who instructs her son, Cupid, to make Psyche fall in love with the ugliest animal in the world. Inevitably, however, Cupid falls in love with her and, rather than carrying out his mother's instructions, carries her off to a mountain. Cupid promises her that, so long as she never sets eyes on him, their relationship will last forever. For a time this arrangement works, but Psyche gradually gets lonely and persuades Cupid to allow her to bring her sisters to visit her. The sisters arrive and, prompted by their jibes about her invisible husband, she resolves to try and see him. Lighting candles one night, she immediately recognises him but, with her hand unsteady, wax drops on Cupid who wakes immediately. He flees, leaving Psyche distraught. She pleads for Juno and Ceres to intercede on her behalf, but to no avail. Eventually she presents herself to Juno, who sets her a number of well-nigh impossible tasks, culminating in the bringing of a flask of the water of youth from Proserpina in the Underworld. She is warned that on no account must she open the flask, but she ignores the imprecation and falls into a trance. During this time Cupid has been pleading with Jupiter to permit him to marry Psyche lawfully. Jupiter eventually agrees and Cupid wakes Psyche with the tip of one of his arrows. The pair marry and Psyche is reconciled with Venus; Jupiter himself passes her the phial of Nectar that will guarantee her eternal life.

Pyramus and Thisbe Another relatively late addition to the legendary world, the story of the lovers Pyramus and Thisbe is first told by Ovid. The ill-starred love story is used by Shakespeare as the play within the play of *A Midsummer Night's Dream* and there are distinct overtones of the later story of Romeo and Juliet in the tale. According to Ovid, the parents of the two lovers refused to allow them to marry, but despite this they were still able to talk. They agreed to meet at a mulberry bush near to the tomb of Ninus. However, Thisbe arrived first and instead

ABOVE: Rape of Proserpina, by Pieter Mulier, also known as 'Cavaliere Tempesta'. Christie's Images

of Pyramus met a lion and, running away, lost her veil. Pyramus arriving later found the veil covered in blood and believed that his lover was dead. Distraught, he commits suicide, whereupon Thisbe then finds his body. She then also commits suicide. The result of this is that the fruit of the mulberry, which had been white up until that point, becomes red in the future.

Quirinus One of the oldest of all Roman gods, Quirinus was probably a war god of the Sabines. The Quirinal Hill was probably named after him. His festival was held on 17 February. However, his importance declined with the rise of Mars as the war god. There are some indications that Quirinus was a deity derived from Romulus.

Rhea Silvia There are a number of legends about the origins of Romulus and Remus, the founders of Rome. Rhea Silvia was according to tradition the daughter of Numitor, the king of Alba Longa. In this version of the foundation story, Numitor is overthrown by his brother Amulius, who forces Rhea Silvia to become a Vestal Virgin in the hope of ensuring that there is no threat to his usurpation of the throne through Rhea Silvia's relationship with Mars. However, Rhea Silvia becomes pregnant and as a result she and her twin boys are thrown into the Tiber. Romulus and Remus are rescued.

Romulus and Remus According to legend, Rome was founded by twin brothers, Romulus (after whom Rome was supposed to have been called) and Remus. The legend was that the twins, the grandsons of Numitor king of Alba Longa, were the sons of Rhea Silvia and the god Mars. Prior to their birth Numitor had been deposed by his brother Amulius, who, to protect himself, made Rhea Silvia a Vestal Virgin. Following the birth the twins were thrown into the River Tiber from where they were rescued and then suckled by a she-wolf, finally they are brought up by a shepherd and his wife. Growing to maturity, they kill Amulius and restore Numitor to his throne before departing to found their own city. Remus was eventually killed by Romulus after the former had crossed a sacred earthwork built by his brother. The Roman historian Livy ascribed the foundation of Rome to the year 753BC and the motif of the she-wolf suckling the two baby twins has been found on coinage dating from the second half of the third century BC.

Sabines The Sabines were a race that lived to the east of Rome. According to tradition a group of Sabines were the original inhabitants of the settlement built on the Quirinal Hill in Rome. Also according to legend the rape of the Sabine women, a theme that was much explored in western art, was one of the episodes in the life of Romulus, when he and a band of followers abducted a group of Sabine girls. The Sabines were finally defeated by Rome in 299BC and Romanised shortly thereafter.

Salus An old Roman goddess of welfare and security, Salus came to be regarded as the equivalent of the Greek god Hygeia. She is normally portrayed holding a cup in one hand and a serpent in the other. It was common practice for Roman matrons to dedicate their cut-off hair to her.

Sarapis An example of a Egyptian god that came to have a cult in Rome, Sarapis was a god of healing. A temple dedicated to him existed in Rome from the 1st century BC, but his cult was gradually overtaken by another import from Egypt, the cult of Isis.

Saturn The Saturnalia, held annually on 17 December, was the greatest festival of the agricultural year and links Saturn, about whom little is really known for certain, into agrarian life. It is probable that he was linked with sowing. To Romans he was related to the Greek god Cronos, the father of Zeus, and, therefore, in Roman terms the father of Jupiter. The Saturnalia was one of the most important Roman festivals in the calendar and one in which, unusually, slaves were permitted to take part.

Sibyl Originally there was only one Sibyl, a prophetess who lived near Troy, but classical literature gradually expands the number. Of the known Sibyls, one of the most famous is the Cumaean Sibyl, who guides Aeneas through the Underworld in Virgil's *Aeneid*. According to legend, this Sibyl also possessed nine books of prophecies, which she offered to sell to Tarquinius Priscus, the last king of Rome. He refused to buy them, whereupon she destroys three and offers him the remaining six at the original price. Again he declines the offer and she burns three more. She then offers the three remaining volumes at the same price; this time Tarquinius accepts the offer. These volumes were then preserved and used as a reference by the senate until their destruction in 83BC.

Silvanus Son of a shepherd and a goat, Silvanus was a god of gardens and woodland. Portrayed with the body of a man and the legs of a goat, he can also (like Faunus) be seen as the equivalent of the Greek deity Pan.

Sol Linked to the agricultural year, Sol, the god of sun, was initially a relatively unimportant deity despite the importance of sun in the growth of crops. The development of his importance occurred under the increasing influence of oriental religions and under the Emperor Diocletian (who reigned from AD284 until his abdication and retirement in AD305) the cult of Sol was raised to one of the most important in the state.

Somnus The Roman god of sleep can be seen as the equivalent of the Greek god Hypnos, who was the son of Nyx (the god of night). To the Greeks Hypnos lives, in one version of the legend, in a cave on the island of Lemnos

Spartacus Few who have seen the film Spartacus can fail to be moved by the dramatic story of the Thracian gladiator who escaped from his training camp at Capua with 70 colleagues and raised the spectre of popular rebellion against the Roman state. Numerous slaves followed him and at the height of the rebellion some 90,000 men were under his command. The armies of Rome were defeated in battle, but the rebellion was to end in defeat and tragedy when, in 71BC, Crassus defeated the rebel army. Unlike the film, where Spartacus was crucified, in history he was to fall on the battlefield; many of his followers were, however, to feel the full pitiless weight of Roman retribution.

Tarpeia The Tarpeian Rock — a cliff on the south-west face of the Capitol — was the location from which traitors and conspirators were thrown off. The legend behind the Tarpeian Rock was that Tarpeia, the daughter of a Roman commander, was so greedy that she was prepared to allow the Sabines to capture the city in exchange for their gold bracelets. Rather than hand these over, however, the Sabines killed her with their shields.

ABOVE: Bronze bust of Silenus. Son of Pan or Hermes, Silenus is the companion and tutor of the wine-god Dionysus. Despite his Greek origins, he was often seen in Roman art. Christie's Images

Tellus An old Roman goddess of earth, Tellus had a festival — the Fordicidia — celebrated on 15 April when a cow in calf was sacrificed to her. Tellus was the Roman equivalent of Gaia. Gaia was one of the first to be born from Chaos in the creation myth alongside Erebus (darkness), Nyx (night) and Tartarus (the underworld). Gaia is the mother of Uranus (the sky) and Pontus (the sea). She is then the consort of Uranus with whom she conceives the 12 Titans. Cronos is the youngest of these; he defies Uranus and castrates him. The blood of Uranus then falls on Gaia and impregnates her with the Furies, the giants and the nymphs. It is Gaia, when Cronos (Saturn) proves to be a tyrant, that ensures that Zeus (Jupiter) survives to overcome his father. Gaia objects to the imprisonment of Cronos and the other Titans. Following a relationship with Tartarus, the monsters Titan and Echidna are born, who rebels against Zeus but are defeated. According to myth, it was Gaia that provided the first oracle at Delphi, but her cult gradually declines in importance through antiquity to be replaced by those of, for example, Demeter.

Tiberius Step-son of Caesar Augustus and son of Livia (who married in 38BC), Tiberius Julius Caesar Augustus was born in 42BC. A successful military leader, he was only adopted as Augustus's heir presumptive in AD4. Following Augustus's death in AD14 Tiberius succeeded him. He was already, by Roman standards an elderly man, and his long reign was marked by efficient administration — unlike most of the emperors he actually bequeathed a treasury with money in it rather than debts. He was, however, a deeply hated man, particularly amongst the aristocracy and senate, and much of his reign was marked by campaigns against individuals and by internecine strife amongst members of the imperial family. In AD26 he established himself on the island of Capri, off the coast at Naples, from where he endeavoured to rule the empire. It was on the island of Capri that, according to Roman historians like Suetonius in his *The Twelve Caesars*, Tiberius behaved in a most licentious and debauched fashion. These tales are probably distorted, but do reflect the hatred and distrust that Tiberius generated. Despite this, however, Tiberius was (unusually for a Roman emperor) to die a natural death in AD37.

Venus Regarded as the Roman equivalent of the Greek god Aphrodite and thus the lover of Mars (in parallel with Aphrodite's relationship with Aries), Venus was a goddess of fertility. She was believed to be a bringer of luck and as such was popular amongst certain generals. In order to legitimise their position, the imperial family, from Julius Caesar through Augustus onwards, claimed that their family had its origins in Aeneas, who, according to legend, was the son of Aphrodite.

Bronze statuette of Venus Pudica.
Christie's Images

Verginia A heroine of the early days of Rome, Verginia was killed by her father, Verginius, rather than allow her to be defiled by the tyrant Appius Claudius. When her body was exposed to the public, it caused a popular uprising that led to the defeat of the Decemviri (a board of 10 members that ruled Rome from 451BC).

Victoria The Roman equivalent of Nike, Victoria was the goddess of victory and was popular with and primarily worshipped (inevitably) by the army. In Greek

Marble statue of Venus.
Christie's Images

myth Nike was supposed to be the daughter of the Titan Pallas, but supported the Olympian gods in their struggle against Cronos. It is Nike that accompanies Hercules to Olympus after he is deified. She is normally portrayed with huge wings flying at great speed to aid the victory of those favoured by the gods. It was her altar in the senate in Rome that witnessed one of the last struggles in the city between the Christians and the pagans when in AD382 the altar was removed on the orders of the Emperor Gratian. A campaign, led by Quintus Aurelius Symmachus was unsuccessful in its demands for the altar's restoration.

Volupta Regarded as the daughter of Cupid and Psyche, Volupta was a goddess of pleasure.

Vulcan The Italian god of fire came to be associated with the Greek god Hephaestus. According to one Greek legend he was the son of Zeus and Hera (ie Jupiter and Juno to Romans), but was born misshapen and was cast aside by Hera. He was rescued from the sea and became an expert blacksmith before being returned to Olympus by his mother where he wrought wondrous works, including the armour that protected Achilles. He was married to Aphrodite, but was exposed to ridicule by the other gods when he sought to expose her adultery with Aries. Because Vulcan was associated with fire and volcanoes — hence the modern word volcanology meaning the study of volcanoes — his temples were always placed outside cities for safety. An annual festival, the Volcanalia, was held every 23 August.

The Vestal Virgins Vesta was the Roman goddess of the hearth and was one of the many household gods. Initially her cult was primarily domestic, but with the growth of the cult of the king, the royal hearth came to have greater significance. Surviving in Rome, at the Forum Boarium, is a circular temple dedicated to Vesta (it is said that the temple was modelled on the hut of Romulus). Here an eternal flame was kept alight by the goddess's priestesses, the Vestal Virgins (the Vestales). The Vestal Virgins, who normally numbered six, were selected by the Pontifex Maximum. Although they were highly honoured and served for 30 years (after which they could marry), they could also be severely punished if they allowed the eternal flame to die and could be buried alive if they forgot their vow of chastity. According to legend, the mother of Romulus and Remus, Rhea Silvia, was made into a Vestal Virgin by her uncle Amulius when he deposed her father from the throne of Alba Longa.

RIGHT: Venus demanding arms for Achilles from the forge of Vulcan by Jacques Blanchard. Christie's Images

LEFT and FAR LEFT: The Forum in Rome. Although in ruins the scale of the remaining monuments and stones leave an imposing impression of the might of Rome. The Forum was built and inhabited for 12 centuries and was the centre of the Empire and Republic in political, religious and commercial terms. The buildings were left to decay after the fall of the Roman Empire until they were excavated in the 19th and 20th centuries.
Life-File/Mike Evans

BELOW: The east-facing Basilica is the oldest temple at Paestum, dating from mid 6BC. It contains 50 barrel-shaped, fluted Doric columns and the remains of a sacrificial altar at the entrance.
Peter Kamara

Chronological Table

753BC	Rome founded
753-509BC	Rule of the Roman Kings
509BC	Republic Declared
499BC	Romans beat Latins at Lake Regillus
390BC	Sack of Rome by Gauls
334-264BC	Conquest of Italy
333-323BC	Alexander the Great dominates the known world
264-241BC	First Punic War
218-202BC	Second Punic War; Hannibal crosses Alps and defeats Rome at Lake Trasemene 217; ends at Battle of Zama 202
202-191BC	Conquest of Cisalpine Gaul
146BC	Greece becomes a Roman province
88-79BC	Sulla dictator
73-71BC	Revolt of Spartacus
60BC	The First Triumvirate — Pompey, Crassus and Julius Caesar
58-51BC	Caesar's conquest of Gaul; expedition to Britain
49-44BC	Civil War; Caesar crosses Rubicon 49; made Dictator for life 44
44BC	Ides of March(15/3) Caesar assassinated
43BC	The Second Triumvirate — Octavius, Lepidus and Mark Anthony
40-30BC	War between Octavius and Mark Anthony
27BC	Augustus(Octavius) becomes Emperor following defeat of Mark Anthony at Actium
43AD	Roman occupation of Britain
64AD	Great fire of Rome
66-73AD	Jewish revolt. Temple destroyed in 70. Masada falls 73
79AD	Eruption of Vesuvius; Colisseum dedicated
117-138AD	Reign of Hadrian
122AD	Hadrian's Wall begun
306-337AD	Reign of Constantine; adoption of Christianity as state religion
410AD	Alaric the Visigoth sacks Rome
455AD	Rome sacked by Vandals
476AD	Deposition of last Emperor in the west — Romulus Augustus
540AD	Byzantine reconquest of Italy by Justinian
1453AD	Fall of Constantinopole to Turks

A Roman marble statue of the Trojan prince Paris. The Romans believed they were descended from the Trojans through the lineage of Aeneas.
Christie's Images